Studies in Mediaeval History

Edited by Geoffrey Barraclough

MEDIAEVAL GERMANY
911 — 1250

This Series, intended in the first place for students in the Universities, is designed to provide a collection of works of moderate compass, in which the reader will find a synthesis of recent historical research. It is not a series of text-books, but a collection of studies, and its object is less to furnish an outline of facts, than to help the student to understand the major problems of mediaeval history. Discussion and explanation, rather than narrative, is its purpose. In this way it is hoped that the series may serve to fill the serious gap between the text-books and the learned monographs and articles in which English and continental scholars of the present day are re-writing mediaeval history.

I—2. Mediaeval Germany. *Essays by German historians, translated with an introduction by* G. BARRACLOUGH. 2 *Vols. Introduction*, 7s. 6d. *net, Essays*, 12s. 6d. *net.*

3. Church, State and Christian Society at the time of the Investiture Contest. *By* G. TELLENBACH, *Professor in the University of Giessen. Translated by* R. F. BENNETT, *Fellow of Magdalene College, Cambridge.* [*In preparation.*]

4. Kingship, Law, and Constitution in the Middle Ages. *By* F. KERN, *Professor in the University of Bonn. Translated by* S. B. CHRIMES, *Lecturer in the University of Glasgow.* [*In preparation.*]

MEDIAEVAL GERMANY

911 — 1250

Essays by German Historians

Translated with an Introduction
by GEOFFREY BARRACLOUGH

Volume I
INTRODUCTION

BASIL BLACKWELL
OXFORD
1938

Printed in Great Britain for Basil Blackwell & Mott Ltd.
at The Vincent Works in the City of Oxford

PREFACE

THE object of the present work is to make it possible for English readers, particularly students of mediaeval history in the Universities, to know something of the important contributions which modern German historians have made in recent years to the history of mediaeval Germany. The work was first planned as long ago as 1935, and was a direct result of experience acquired as a teacher of mediaeval history in Oxford and subsequently in Cambridge. I found, when I began to teach in Oxford, that the paucity of English works on mediaeval Europe imposed serious limitations on the teacher, and made it very difficult to recommend reading which offered more than either a superficial or else an antiquated point of view. I found, in particular, that it was almost impossible to put students in touch with the vital questions on which European historical scholarship is concentrated at the present day, and therefore difficult to awaken the interest which such questions might be expected to arouse in informed and intelligent pupils. There were many issues which were literally unknown to a majority of students, and which were bound to remain unknown, unless they could be brought face to face with the work of modern continental scholars. And the biggest gaps of all were in the history of Germany. It was rare to have to deal with a pupil unable to make use of French authorities, but those who were in a position to study the work of German historians were perhaps rarer still. It therefore seemed to me that there was a pressing necessity to restore the balance by trans-

v

lating at least a representative selection of the more outstanding work produced by German historians in recent years.

The present volumes on " Mediaeval Germany " are a first result of this endeavour. I have deliberately chosen to translate a series of essays, because it seems to me that, where so little is known of the views of modern German historians, and of their attitude to the problems of German history, eight different points of view are bound to be more illuminating than one. On the other hand, the essays have been carefully selected to present a coherent and consecutive account of German history from the tenth to the thirteenth century, a picture of what German historians call, in GIESEBRECHT's phrase, the *Kaiserzeit*. Some students may nevertheless feel that they need a broader and more elementary background, if they are to derive full profit from the works translated. Such a background I have tried to supply in a long introductory essay, written in the summer and autumn of 1937. The reader will see not only that my essay links together the essays translated, but also that it sorts out for English readers certain phases and problems of German history, on which the attention of English historians has long been concentrated. These questions are re-examined in the light of recent research and re-interpretation, and the first volume thus provides an introduction to some of the more outstanding German historical work of recent years which, because of its length or technicality or for other reasons, could not be included in the second volume.

From the days of Otto the Great to the time of Henry III and, indeed, down to the end of the reign of Barbarossa, Germany was the strongest and most stable power in Europe, and German history therefore naturally assumes a predominant place in European history. In view of this fact, the dearth of modern books on mediaeval Germany in the English language is remarkable, and this lack makes it difficult to give the student a balanced perception of the history of mediaeval Europe as a whole. The present work, in which particular attention has been paid to those aspects of German internal development which lend themselves to comparison with France and England, should make it easier to approach the history of Germany with the same sense of reality with which we approach the history of mediaeval England or of mediaeval France, and so enable the student to adopt that comparative point of view which engenders an understanding of the organic differences in the development of the great European states. Nevertheless, it is a history of Germany, and not of the Empire, and its main theme is the internal development of the German state. To have introduced that most controversial of subjects, the mediaeval Empire, would have altered the whole plan of the present work, in which constitutional questions have been deliberately placed in the foreground. There is no constitutional history of Germany in the English language; and it is this gap which the present volumes are intended primarily to fill. If the present work is sufficiently successful to justify a continuation, I should wish later to publish in the same series a further volume, in which some of the more recent literature on the Empire, and on imperial and Italian policy, can be put before English readers. Here also, lack of knowledge of modern research and reinterpretation is a serious drawback for English students.

In selecting essays for translation I have had one further object before me. My aim was not merely to provide chapters on consecutive aspects of German history, but also to illustrate the various methods of approach which German scholars have adopted. The reader will therefore find that the essays in the second volume of this work have certain merits as an introduction to different historical methods, apart from any merit which they may possess as studies of German history. There is, for example, a striking example of the use of the tried methods of German " diplomatic ", of the close and accurate interpretation of documentary evidence, which has been the pride of German scholarship since the days of SICKEL and FICKER; but there are also studies which subordinate documentary evidence to " geo-political " considerations, and to such factors as the evidence of place-names or the deductions which can be drawn from the spread of colonization. There are studies which begin with social history, the history of classes, and there are studies in which economic history predominates. The inter-relationship of political history and the history of thought and ideas is illustrated; and there is more than one study of legal history. An insight into the methods of German historians, it seemed to me, might be valuable to English historians working in their own field of study, quite apart from the new knowledge of the history of Germany in which such methods have resulted. But this purpose has remained subordinate, and in every case I have made it my aim only to select for translation essays which—whatever their method of approach—contributed directly to an understanding of German history as a whole. It would be too much to expect that the selection should meet with universal approbation. Every historian will be able to think of essays which he would desire to see included. But the reader may be assured that the difficult task of selection has been the subject of long and careful consideration, and that I have spared no pains to secure representative work. The volume sets out to provide an introduction to German historical work of the present century which—as I have tried to show in my introductory essay—has revised many of the standard views of nineteenth-century writers; but I have done my best to avoid what the next generation of historians, looking back to 1938, may perhaps be tempted to describe simply as " novelties ". Some of the work translated reaches back to pre-war days, and I have not been dissuaded from including one classic essay which was composed in 1894—the essay by ULRICH STUTZ, which the author was able to correct and approve before his untimely death in July, 1938. In my own introductory essay, on the other hand, no attempt has been made to refer to more than what seemed to me to be the more important German monographs of recent years: references to the great handbooks of German history—WAITZ, for example, or HAUCK or SCHRÖDER—are only exceptionally included.

It only remains for me to acknowledge my obligations, and not least my indebtedness to the Warden and Fellows of Merton College, without whose support I could hardly have undertaken this work. I cannot mention by name all those who have kindly given me advice and information, but the generous help of Professor P. E. Schramm must be singled out, and I must further express my gratitude to my wife for undertaking the heavy task of preparing the indices. Various parts of the manuscript have been read by Professor P. H. Winfield and by Professor W. Levison, and the whole has been read by Mr. E. S. Cohn, Fellow of Brasenose College, whose interest in my work, extending now over more than a dozen years, has provided the stimulus which alone emboldened me to undertake this task. Finally, Mr. H. L. Schollick, who has been in charge of the publication, has given me constant advice and invaluable critical help. My greatest debt, however, is necessarily to the eight German and Austrian historians who have generously allowed me to translate their works, and have given me all the help in the task which I have desired. In many cases, they have facilitated my work by slight modification and revision for the purposes of an English edition; and to them, and to their publishers in Germany, whose permission to translate is acknowledged separately, my special thanks are due. If the present volumes contribute to making their work better known and more widely appreciated in England, it may be some compensation for the kindness and patience they have shown throughout the many months in which I have been engaged on the task of translation.

G. B.

CONTENTS

xi

ABBREVIATIONS

D (DO. II, DH. III, etc.) = Monumenta Germaniae historica, Diplomata regum et imperatorum Germaniae (DH. III = Diplomata Heinrici III).

HG. = H. Hirsch, Die Hohe Gerichtsbarkeit im deutschen Mittelalter (Prag, 1922).

HZ. = Historische Zeitschrift.

JL. = Ph. Jaffé, Regesta Pontificum Romanorum (ed. alt., ed. S. Loewenfeld, F. Kaltenbrunner, P. Ewald, Lipsiae, 1885—1888).

Lr. u. Sg. = H. Mitteis, Lehnrecht und Staatsgewalt. Untersuchungen zur mittelalterlichen Verfassungsgeschichte (Weimar, 1933).

MG. = Monumenta Germaniae historica.
　Const. = Constitutiones et acta publica imperatorum et regum.
　Epp. = Epistolae.
　in us. schol. = Scriptores rerum Germanicarum in usum scholarum.
　Lib. de lite = Libelli de lite imperatorum et pontificum saec. XI. et XII. conscripti.
　Script. = Scriptores.

MIÖG. = Mitteilungen des Instituts für österreichische Geschichtsforschung.

St. = K. F. Stumpf, Die Reichskanzler, Vol. II: Die Kaiserurkunden des X., XI. und XII. Jahrhunderts chronologisch verzeichnet (Innsbruck, 1865—1883).

ZRG. = Zeitschrift der Savigny-Stiftung für Rechtsgeschichte (*Germ. Abt.* = Germanistische Abteilung; *Kanon. Abt.* = Kanonistische Abteilung).

THE BACKGROUND OF GERMAN HISTORY: EMPIRE AND PAPACY

THE following pages are intended to serve as an introduction to German constitutional history in the period of the Saxon, Salian and Hohenstaufen emperors, and their first object is to provide a background for the series of essays and studies by distinguished German historians which together form the second volume of this history. Readers who already know the main lines of German constitutional development in the first great era of German history will have no difficulty in following the arguments and appreciating the significance of the essays here selected for translation; but others may welcome an introductory attempt by an English writer to interpret for English readers the main currents of German historical scholarship in the last thirty years and to link the essays which follow, with each other, and with other outstanding historical work which, because of its length or detail or for other reasons, it has not been possible to translate.

Without any revolution and equally without any desertion of the high standards set by nineteenth-century German scholarship, there has without doubt been a reorientation of German historical work in the last generation, as interesting in its methods as in its results: interest is concentrated more on Germany itself, for example, than (as in the days of GIESEBRECHT) on the Empire; without contesting the achievement of Otto the Great, emphasis has been transferred to the period of reconstruction after the Investiture Contest; the interaction of economic and constitutional development is better understood; and more attention is given to the growth of the local powers with which the Hohenstaufen monarchy had to contend. Similarly, also, the relations of church and state were seen in a new light after the publication of ULRICH STUTZ's classic essay on the *Eigenkirche* in 1895.[1] Thus, without leaving the old framework, a new interpretation has gradually been placed on the process of German development—an interpretation often helped, as in the work of HEINRICH MITTEIS[2] or PERCY SCHRAMM[3], by comparison with England and France. To ignore this scholarship is like ignoring the work of MAITLAND, STENTON, TOUT or JOLLIFFE and reading English history from the pages of KEMBLE, STUBBS, FREEMAN or GREEN: the result may not be wrong, but it is necessarily one-sided and—where recent research has revealed new forces at play and new under-currents of social life—equally necessarily superficial, for each generation sets itself new problems in its exploration of the past and the answers of nineteenth-century historians can no longer satisfy, not because they are necessarily wrong, but because they answer questions which are no longer vital.[4]

[1] *Infra* II, 35—70; cf. also U. Stutz, *Gesch. d. kirchlichen Benefizialwesens von seinen Anfängen bis auf Alexander III* (1895).

[2] *Lehnrecht u. Staatsgewalt* (1933); cf. *infra* II, 235—279.

[3] In his studies on the history of the coronation ceremonies; cf. the list in Schramm, *A History of the English Coronation* (1937), 239—240.

[4] Cf. for example, B. Schmeidler, *infra* II, 72, and Th. Mayer, *infra* II, 175; and see particularly the concluding remarks in Hans Hirsch's important book, *Die hohe Gerichtsbarkeit im deutschen Mittelalter* (Prag, 1922), 237: " It has long been recognized that in Germany everything connected with and leading to the modern state . . . developed along provincial lines, in contrast to France and England . . . The answer to the question, what were the causes of this difference, will hardly be so simple as . . . has been supposed: i.e., that the German rulers, diverted by continuous negotiations with the papacy and by their position in Italy

The following pages are therefore an attempt at reinterpretation in the light of more recent German scholarship: they are an introduction to the history of mediaeval Germany as it is seen by German historians of the present when they seek to create a living picture from the more specialized and detailed work of the last thirty years. There can, of course, be no question of covering the whole field of German constitutional life between the days of Henry I and Frederick II. But there are certain main topics—the duchies, the monarchy, the church, the counties and the principalities—which constitute the framework within which German development took place, and a re-examination of the problems connected with them is necessary as the first step towards a better understanding of German history as a whole. So long as the development of the German people is measured by outworn standards, so long as factors are emphasized which no longer loom so large as they did in the closing years of the nineteenth century, if there is a mistaken formulation of questions and an unrealistic conception of historical potentialities, the significance of German history must remain obscure and interest in its problems be diminished. Such, in the main, is the position in England to-day; and it is therefore not surprising that a leading German historian has described the only recent book on mediaeval Germany in the English language as a synthesis of " yesterday's scholarship ", a reflection of the twilight of a day which has passed.[5] Tied to

and Burgundy, gave way to the demands of the aristocracy at precisely the moment when, if the central government were to be strengthened, a directly contrary policy was necessary. To emphasize such considerations is not incorrect; but they are only the external aspect of the problem.''

[5] Cf. B. Schmeidler, HZ. CXL (1929), 592: ". . . Aber der deutsche Forscher, der im Zusammenhang der gegenwärtigen Forschung lebt, würde häufig lieber die Arbeiten von Stutz, Pöschl, Seeliger, Hirsch, Dopsch,

an unreal and visionary imperialism, cut off for ever from the mainsprings of political action, as we see them surging into life in mediaeval England or France, the Germany of the Ottos, the Henrys or the Fredericks seems denuded of all but antiquarian interest, its life lived on another plane from that of the feudal states of Western Europe, its efforts concentrated on the resurrection of a past which was irretrievably dead.

It is against this view of mediaeval Germany as a dim reminiscence of the Carolingian world, devoid of the vital principles which were to form the great feudal states of the thirteenth century—a view which a French scholar has not hesitated to express with categorical and uncompromising logic[6] and which many English historians have implicitly accepted—that recent German historians have rebelled. For them the characteristic feature of German constitutional life in the middle ages is its richness and variety, the vitality of the elements which sprang directly from the soil, the constant flux, the unceasing rise of new factors and re-emergence of old forces. These factors recall in many ways the later phases of Anglo-Saxon civilization, but unlike Anglo-Saxon civilization, which was swamped by the Norman invader, German constitutional life continued, until late in the middle ages, to be dominated by elements which reached back in origin to the primitive society

Waas, Heusinger, Schreiber, Hartmann . . . und vieles andere der Art verwertet finden. . . . Es ist alles ein wenig Wissenschaft von gestern, vielleicht von gestern abend, was da geboten wird, nicht die letzte Feinheit der heutigen Problemstellungen und Gesichtspunkte.''

[6] L. Reynaud, *Les origines de l'influence française en Allemagne* (1913) —a book which has been bitterly criticized (cf. for example C. Erdmann, *Die Entstehung des Kreuzzugsgedankens*, 1935, 56 n. 12), but which is nevertheless solidly based on the results of nineteenth-century German scholarship. However distorted Reynaud's conclusions may be, the more fundamental error lies in the attitude of the writers who provided Reynaud with his material.

which was momentarily hidden by Carolingian uniformity. The strength and vitality of the ancient provincial administration of Anglo-Saxon England, the lathes of Kent, the rapes of Sussex, the shires of the north and the wapentakes of the midlands, are better understood to-day, and it is realized that the hundred organization of the tenth century only superficially superseded the older administrative divisions; but the amalgamation of old and new, the blending and confusion which produced a " bewildering appearance of diversity of size and jurisdiction ",[7] hardly outlasted the Anglo-Saxon period, and from the time of Domesday, at the latest, the tendency to uniformity and standardization was irrevocable and there was never any opportunity for the institutions which sprang from the " folk " to transform the administrative organization superimposed by the crown. In Germany, on the other hand, the same primitive institutions preserve their vitality for another two or even three hundred years; and it is at the end of the twelfth and in the thirteenth century that we find such courts as the *Gogerichte* of Saxony and the *Zehntgerichte* of Alamannia rising to new importance and transforming the organization of provincial jurisdiction.[8]

This element of continuity is clear enough as compared with England and clear even as compared with France, which was, in large part, a demesne conquered by the Capetian dynasty in a way not very different from the Norman conquest of England. It was the continuity of a variety of vital elements and not of one established form of government; and

---

[7] Cf. Jolliffe, *Const. Hist.* (1937), 121—122.
[8] For Saxony, cf. Philippi, MIÖG. XXIX (1908), 225 sqq., and XXXV (1914), 209—259, and HZ. CXXIX (1924), 189—232. In general, cf. Hirsch, HG., 185—203, and in summary, 227—229.

the consequence was that the life which surged up afresh in every element of the constitution from generation to generation prevented, except perhaps under Otto I and his immediate successors, anything which might be called a solution of constitutional problems. German history is therefore dynamic, perhaps in a sense even daemonic: the potentialities are great; the efforts of rulers, kings and princes alike, are strenuous; the forces at play are vast, often incalculable and sometimes inscrutable; and the result, until the very end, is uncertain and almost poignant in its uncertainty. There can be no doubt that the death of Frederick II brought to a close the first period of German history and that the Interregnum between 1250 and 1272 separated the age of emperors from the age of princes. There can be no doubt, moreover, that the transformation which German constitutional life underwent in those fateful years was implicit in much which had gone before:[9] there was no sudden crisis, and if we want to find a real turning-point we must look much further back to the age of Henry IV and Henry V.[10] But the historian who follows Frederick II's German policy step by step, who appreciates his systematic building up of the crown demesne and understands his administrative reforms, will not only realize how far from the truth is the old statement that " Frederick II left Germany to the princes," but will also find it hard, in spite of his knowledge of the débâcle which was to come, to believe that this statesmanlike plan was foredoomed to failure.[11] As late as the

[9] *Infra* II, 265.
[10] Cf. *infra* II, 127, 170—173.
[11] Cf. for example, F. Schneider, *Kaiser Friedrich II. u. der Staat* (1930), and for further literature, *infra*, cap. VI.—E. Kantorowicz, *Frederick the Second* (1931), has little to say on this side of Frederick's policy. For the forces which led to the break up, cf. M. Stimming, " Kaiser Friedrich II. u. der Abfall der deutschen Fürsten," HZ. CXX (1919), 210—249.

first half of the thirteenth century, in other words, the potentialities of the German situation were incalculable. The result might well be what we know it to have been, but it might equally well have been radically different; and the probability is that, if we could take our stand at about the year 1230, we should unhesitatingly condemn as unthinkable the situation which actually came into existence a generation later. Not until 1272, in short, had it become clear which forces were to dominate: then, and not until then, was an equilibrium reached which, in spite of all political fluctuations, was to remain for centuries an almost unchanging constitutional factor in German history. The three earlier centuries, on the other hand, the three hundred years which passed between the first mention of a *regnum Teutonicorum* in the days of Henry I[12] and the reign of Frederick II, were years of continuous constitutional experiment and endeavour; they saw the rise of new forces and the strengthening of old ones; they saw the efforts of the monarchy to cope with these forces; and they saw one programme of constitutional reform and reorganisation follow another, without a final solution being achieved. No constitutional scene is so varied, none so rich and instructive. The very strength of the elements in the constitutional situation means that the historian who is willing to probe below the surface comes more quickly and more directly to the mainsprings of political action in Germany than elsewhere, and the variety of forces whose interplay drives on the stream of constitutional development is the really distinguishing feature of German history and the characteristic which lends it colour and life and individuality.

[12] *Infra* II, 80 n. 6, 236 n. 6.

It is one of the cardinal weaknesses of English histories of mediaeval Germany and one reason why German constitutional history is so little understood and used as material for comparison in England, that not only the unparalleled richness in " autogenous " political forces but also the fluid, organic form of constitutional development which are together characteristic of German public life, are all too apt to be overlooked and ignored. The result is that German constitutional history, so far as it is studied at all, is simplified not only to the point of falsification but also to the point at which all its most characteristic and most interesting features are omitted. The two factors which still receive most emphasis are the influence of the struggle with the Gregorian church, the contest between *imperium* and *sacerdotium*, and—closely related with this—the effects of imperial policy and of the connexion with Italy. Neither of these, however,—profound though its influence may have been—can really be considered a specifically constitutional factor at all: they are factors which influenced the constitutional situation without being part of it. When the German middle ages are considered from a more specifically constitutional point of view, therefore, three further factors are commonly noted: the whole problem, in the first place, which centres round the " stem duchy " or what may more generally be called the federal character of a constitution based on separate tribal or racial units, the elective monarchy which is intimately connected with the federal constitution, and finally the usurpation of royal rights by the baronage.

It must be our first task to consider, without any attempt at completeness, these five factors which are usually regarded as the essential differentiating features of German constitutional development between 911 or 918 and 1250. A full consideration of the first two would take us far beyond the bounds of German history into the widely different sphere of imperial history and—in the case of the church at least—into the broad domain of universal history in which it is scarcely possible, without falsification, to single out one country from the whole community of European lands. There is, indeed, no doubt that both the imperial problem and the relations of empire and papacy are closely entwined in the roots of German history, and it is essential not to underrate the connexion. It might, for instance, be shown that the imperial connexion powerfully stimulated German expansion eastwards and thus furthered the most obviously national movement of the German middle ages.[13] But it is not our present purpose to investigate the problems involved in the history of the empire and the imperial idea. The recent investigations which have done so much to restore proportion to the discussion of the imperial policy of the German emperors might profitably receive greater attention in England;[14] but it is sufficient for our purpose to note that no historian to-day seriously maintains even of Otto III the views formulated by GREGOROVIUS and GIESEBRECHT.[15] Not only has it been established that there was in his day no surrender of German interests, no abject

[13] Cf. Brackmann, " Reichspolitik u. Ostpolitik im frühen Mittelalter," *Sitz.-berichte d. preuss. Akademie, phil.-hist. Kl.*, 1935, and the earlier articles by the same author which are there cited.

[14] It is hoped to devote a later volume in this series to the empire and imperial policy, from Charles the Great onwards. Cf. particularly P. E. Schramm, *Kaiser, Rom. u. Renovatio* (2 vols., 1929).

[15] Cf. Hampe's judicious summary, HZ. CXL (1929) which should be read in conjunction with M. Uhlirz's subsequent constructive work, MIÖG. XLVIII (1934).

submission to a nebulous imperial mission, but it becomes increasingly clear that the empire, in any other sense than German dominion over Italy and Burgundy, was never sufficiently a reality to blot out the immutable facts of the German situation.

The Investiture Contest, on the other hand, was no uniquely imperial and still less a uniquely German problem:[16] it reached to France and it reached to England, and the concordat of Worms, which brought peace to Germany in 1122, was paralleled by the English concordat of 1107, just as there is a marked similarity between the election of Lothar in 1125 and that of Stephen in 1135. Indeed, it has recently been pointed out how closely interconnected were the solutions and compromises achieved in the three countries.[17] It is, therefore, pertinent to ask why the constitutional significance of the struggle with the Hildebrandine church should be set so high in Germany, so low in England. And so again a century later. Innocent III's policy clearly exerted real constitutional significance in the struggle between Philip of Swabia and Otto of Brunswick; but was it without constitutional influence in the England of King John? Did it contribute nothing to the struggle for the charter in and before 1215? Where, in short, lies the difference and where the necessity for a different treatment of the same influence in the two lands? The same question, moreover, can pertinently be asked about the relations of Germany and Italy. It is well, if it is not the whole truth, to regard the mediaeval empire

---

[16] Cf. particularly G. Tellenbach, *Libertas. Kirche und Weltordnung im Zeitalter des Investiturstreites* (1936), which R. F. Bennett is translating under the title: *Church, State and Christian Society at the time of the Investiture Contest*, as vol. III in this series.

[17] *Lr. u. Sg.*, 228—229.

from time to time as an empire pure and simple, and not as a magnificent but " chimerical " attempt to fulfil a " grandiose conception of universal dominion ". It was, in short, an empire among empires, standing side by side in the critical years of the twelfth century with the great dominion to which the name of Angevin Empire has rightly been given. And yet how different is the estimate of the influence on internal history of imperial policy and foreign policy in England and in Germany! The view stated so forcefully and yet so perversely by GEORG VON BELOW[18]—the view (which in a more moderate form is again raising its head)[19] that the Italian " entanglement " sealed the destiny of Germany and " destroyed the German kingship "—is implicitly and wholeheartedly accepted by the majority of English-speaking historians. But it must again be asked whether it was more fateful than the " continental entanglement " on which the Plantagenets expended so much of their time and energy.[20] There is a tendency, in the study of English constitutional history, to forget the ever influential factor of politics and particularly the influence of foreign policy, to slur over the fact, for example, that unless John had been defeated at the battle of Bouvines there would have been no Magna Carta, or that the baronial rising of 1258 was a direct consequence not so much of Henry III's system of domestic government as of the failure of his foreign policy. But in the study of German internal development the tendency is all

---

[18] *Die italienische Kaiserpolitik des deutschen Mittelalters* (1927).

[19] F. Rörig, *Ursachen u. Auswirkungen des deutschen Partikularismus* (1937), 8—12, 15.

[20] The best survey of Anglo-continental military and diplomatic relations in this period is to be found in W. Kienast, *Die deutschen Fürsten im Dienste der Westmächte* (1924–31); cf. also Powicke, *The Loss of Normandy* (1913).

the other way: everything is made to depend on
foreign policy, on the Italian entanglement and on
relations with that mighty foreign power, the papacy,
and a consistent organic growth of the complex of
governmental rights, duties, forms and methods
which we call the constitution is thereby implicitly
denied.

In these few random comparisons between the
attitude taken to English and that adopted towards
German constitutional development I have tried
only to suggest one main direction in which it is
necessary to correct our perspectives. An attempt
to transform the suggestion into a compelling proof
would take us far out of our way. And, more important still, it would probably fail. For we are dealing, in the last analysis, with " imponderables ".
It is possible to limit here, to circumscribe there, to
define and to cut down the margin of possibilities,[21]
but it is the essence of the problem that in the end
each individual historian must decide for himself,
after duly weighing the established facts, precisely
what place ecclesiastical and imperial factors take
in his conception of the development of mediaeval
Germany. Neither is it possible to draw a hard and
fast line between constitutional and political history,
between internal development and foreign policy.
We cannot isolate the constitutional history of Germany and treat it as something independent and self-
existing. It is, on the other hand, equally wide of
the mark to go to the other extreme and deny it a
consistent form and a coherent evolution. The

---

[21] Cf. *infra*, 77, for a striking case—namely, the relations of Barbarossa
and Henry the Lion—in which it has been shown that the influence of
Italian affairs was not so decisive as an earlier generation of historians had
supposed. The Welf-Staufen antithesis, says Spindler (*Die Anfänge des
bayerischen Landesfürstentums*, 190), was " innerdeutsch ".

examples which I have drawn from John's reign offer us, I believe, not only the nearest but also the fairest parallel. The real interest of that reign is the combination of constitutional discontent, clerical and papal antagonism and unsuccessful war and diplomacy to produce the crisis of 1213—1215, and if there is no possible means of determining which of the three factors was decisive, it is hard to escape the conclusion that no event was more immediately and more directly effective than the defeat of Bouvines.[22] But even a historian who laid full emphasis on the military and diplomatic aspect of the situation would not go so far as to depict the constitutional crisis as the exploitation of a defeated monarch by a selfish baronage. He would not, in short, deny the separate existence of vital constitutional factors and reduce the whole crisis to an incident of *Macht-* or *Realpolitik*. An admission of the strength of the influence exerted by foreign and ecclesiastical complications, in other words, does not destroy the validity and the historical value of the constitutional method of approach. It does not destroy it in England and it does not destroy it in Germany. That the German and the English situations in this regard were absolutely parallel is, of course, not true. External influences in German constitutional development reached an intensity which was unknown in England. But if there is a difference in intensity, a difference in degree, substantial similarity is nevertheless evident; and the organisation of public law which is analysed by Eike von Repgow in his *Sachsenspiegel* is no more the opportunist result of ecclesiastical pressure and

[22] Cf. Cartellieri, *Die Schlacht bei Bouvines im Rahmen der europäischen Politik* (1914).

imperial necessity than are the contemporary institutions of English law and government which are described by Eike's contemporary, Bracton, in his treatise *De legibus et consuetudinibus Angliae*. Each is describing a system which is the product of the whole historical past of his land[23]—a system which the church had helped to form and which had necessarily been influenced by the fluctuations of politics, but a system in which tradition, custom, constitutional practice and a strong sense of right were nevertheless predominant.

" Clerical influence ", it has been well said,[24] " never achieved any success worth mention in Germany except as the ally of German faction." With this statement in mind it will be easier to keep a balanced perspective and to avoid neglecting specifically constitutional factors. It is true, for example, that the history of the German monarchy from the election of Rudolf of Rheinfelden in 1077 to the *Deliberatio* of Innocent III in 1200 shows a marked, if fluctuating, recognition and acceptance of clerical demands and standards. But was this a victory for the church alone ? Was it not rather a victory won because the aims of the church and one part at least of the baronage were identical ? " Even without the judgement of the Holy See," a contemporary wrote, even without papal intervention the attitude of the princes to Henry IV was consistent and justified and their claims were substantiated by constitutional law: they might ally with the papacy, but they stood fair and square on their own ground, striving to realize a policy which was their

---

[23] Cf. particularly H. Fehr, " Die Staatsauffassung Eikes v. Repgow," ZRG. *Germ. Abt.* XXXVII (1916).

[24] Cf. E. Rosenstock, *Königshaus u. Stämme in Deutschland zwischen* 911 *u.* 1250 (1914), 222.

own.[25] The alliance of papacy and baronage, both
during the reign of Henry IV and in other subsequent
crises, cannot be denied;[26] but with its recognition
we are at once forced over into the constitutional
field. For if the aims of the papacy can be comprehended from a clerical and political point of view,
the objects of the other partner in the alliance, the
aims of the baronage, were constitutional in the
fullest sense and demand strictly constitutional interpretation. It was no accident that it was in Germany
alone that the dominant element of the aristocracy
entered wholeheartedly into the papal alliance; and
since it was no accident, it is necessary to enquire
what were the motives which separated the German
baronage from their natural leader, Henry IV, at
a time when Henry I of England could rely on the
support of the English baronage against the pretensions of the Gregorian church. It is an admitted
fact that the German princes could use, and did use,
the papal alliance; but why they used it, why it
played so large a part in their politics as compared,
for example, with England, is another question, and
this question can only be solved by a realistic consideration of the constitutional situation. The constitutional historian, in short, must be prepared to
note and to attempt to weigh the influence of ecclesiastical and imperial policy when he sees it at work;

[25] Paul of Bernried, *Vita Greg.* VII, c. 97: " Praeterea liberi homines
Henricum eo pacto sibi praeposuerunt in regem, ut electores suos iuste
iudicare et regali providentia gubernari satageret. Quod pactum ille postea
praevaricari et contemnere non cessavit, videlicet quoslibet innoxios
tyrannica crudelitate opprimendo et omnes, quos potuit, christianae re-
ligioni repugnare constringendo. Ergo et absque sedis apostolicae iudicio
principes eum pro rege merito refutare possent, cum pactum adimplere
contempserit, quod eis pro electione sua promiserat: quo non adimpleto,
nec rex esse poterat. Nam rex nullatenus esse poterit, qui subditos suos
non regere sed in errorem mittere studuerit." Cf. F. Kern, *Gottesgnadentum
u. Widerstandsrecht* (1914), 202–3, 265.

[26] Cf. *infra* II, 114, 153, 169, 170.

but he must realize that both influences were only effective because the constitutional situation allowed them to be effective, that it was the even balance of constitutional forces which opened the door to external factors. There were specific reasons why German constitutional evolution, as compared with that of England or of France, was particularly susceptible to external influence; but these reasons can only be discovered by a close analysis of the constitutional situation at any particular moment or, more generally, by a careful study of the whole process of constitutional growth. To explain the centrifugal influence of feudalism in Germany by the fact that " the German king's hands were bound by the political situation,"[27] to explain the contrast between France and Germany which is so marked at the middle of the thirteenth century by a " neglect which was forced on the king because the burdens of Italian policy alienated him from his royal duties,"[28] still leaves us without an answer to the ultimate question: why ? Why was the political situation, which was certainly no worse and to all appearance much more favourable in Germany and the empire than in France before the irretrievable failure of King John in his struggles with Philip Augustus,[29]

[27] Rörig, *Partikularismus*, 13.
[28] *Ibid.*, 15.
[29] When Rörig (p. 13) writes that, because the political situation tied the hands of the German king, the German feudatories " gestalten . . . das Lehnrecht, während in Frankreich König und Kronjuristen dasselbe Lehnrecht meisterhaft für den königlichen Staat auszunutzen verstehen," he seems—apart from all doubts as to the justification for his use of the word " dasselbe "—to ignore this fact. The work of the French " crown lawyers " hardly begins before the second half of the thirteenth century (Kern, *Die Anfänge der französischen Ausdehnungspolitik*, 37 sqq.), and—given the successes of Philip Augustus—the " masterly manipulation " of feudalism by his successors and their " jurists " is not difficult to explain. The situation is very different, on the other hand, before 1214 or 1204, and what has to be explained is the success, in spite of the unfavourable political situation, of the earlier Capetians, who provided Philip Augustus with a foundation on which to build. Because he ignores this essential

so fateful to the German rulers and so favourable to
the Capetians ? Why were the German king's hands
bound by a political situation which seems to have
stimulated the French monarchy to action ? Why,
to return to the example with which we began, was
Gregory VII able to intervene so much more freely
in German affairs than in those of France and
England ?

There may be many elements in the answers to
these probing questions, and in a sense they may be
questions to which no ultimate answer is possible.
But it is safe—and, more important, it is high time—
to say that it is from the constitutional situation
that we will get our best indication of the final
answer.[30] There are still too many historians unable
to resist the easy solution of attributing the collapse
of the German monarchy to an unholy fate which
not only threw the irresistible but chimerical attrac-
tions of Italy and world dominion in the way of
Otto I but also robbed the land, at every moment
of crisis, of the strong leader and continuous tradition
which it needed. There is still, in short, a powerful
attraction in contrasting the unbroken Capetian
succession with the misfortunes, calamities and sudden deaths which beset the German royal dynasties.[31]
At no point is this more apparent than at the crisis
of 1198. Henry VI, it is averred, died with the world
at his feet. All problems were on the point of
solution:[32] Italy, papal relations, a hereditary mon-

distinction between the two periods in Capetian history, Rörig's comparison with France is unconvincing.

[30] As regards the factors favouring Gregory VII's intervention, cf.
particularly Hirsch's study, *infra* II, 131—173.

[31] Cf. among many D. Schäfer, "Deutschland als Wahlreich,"
Preussische Jahrbücher CXCVI (1914), 237–8, and in summary Fr. Schnei-
der, *Neuere Anschauungen d. deutschen Historiker z. Beurteilung d. deutschen
Kaiserpolitik d. Mittelalters* (2nd ed., 1936), 22—23.

[32] Cf. for example the relatively judicious judgement of Hampe,

B

archy and fundamental constitutional issues such as the royal right to retain escheats, which would have enabled the German monarchy to build up its demesne as the Capetians were doing and were to do more successfully still in the succeeding century.[33] With Henry VI's early and unexpected death, it is said, the whole mighty structure toppled to the ground, never—in spite of all Frederick II's efforts—to be raised again to its old lofty grandeur. If I dwell on this single event, it is because others have emphasized it so constantly. It is, for many, the great turning point in German history: if Henry had lived all would have been well, because he died the work of the Hohenstaufen was brought to nothing. But if we take as our comparison, instead of the progress of primogeniture in France, the history of the English monarchy, it is at once clear how forced is the contrast, how exaggerated the attempt to tie the fate of Germany to the fate of its ruling dynasty. In England the Conqueror was succeeded in 1087 by his third son, although the eldest son, Robert, was living and was still alive when his younger brother, Henry, succeeded in 1100. In 1135 there is the notorious change of dynasty and Matilda and her son are passed over; but even so, the successful claimant, Stephen, is only a cadet of the house of Blois, with two elder brothers surviving. The dynasty changes again in 1154, although Stephen has an heir,[34] and not until 1189 do we get unques-

Meister der Politik (ed. Marcks & Müller) I (2nd ed.), 666.—The best study of Henry VI's policy generally is E. Perels, *Der Erbreichsplan Heinrichs VI* (1927).

[33] Cf. H. Mitteis, *Politische Prozesse des früheren Mittelalters in Deutschland u. Frankreich* (1927) for a contrast of the effects of the forfeiture of Henry the Lion's fiefs on the one hand, and of John's Norman lands on the other.

[34] It is, however, interesting to note that the hereditary principle was saved, after Eustace's death, by Stephen's adoption of Henry II; but the fact remains that Stephen's own son, William, was still alive.

tioning acceptance of the succession of the eldest
surviving son of the dead king—Richard I, an
absentee king who was as engrossed in " chimerical
dreams " and foreign entanglements as any German
emperor. But 1199 again saw a disputed succession
and the raising of the acute point of law which was
figuring large in contemporary Germany, the relations of uncle and nephew, of John and Arthur of
Brittany—a problem which was only different from
the incipient issue between Philip of Swabia and
Frederick of Sicily because Philip's conscientious
observance of constitutional law prevented his as-
suming full imperial rights and so weakened his
position against the usurping Welf.[35] If any one
factor is decisive in the German situation in 1198,
it is not the lack of an adult heir of the body, but the
strong sense of constitutional right which prevented
Philip from grasping at the substance of power as
John grasped at it in England: if Philip had ignored the claims of Frederick and immediately
accepted the kingship instead of trying to exercise
a regency which was unknown to constitutional law
and unworkable,[36] Germany—though it might not
have been spared a Welf claimant—would assuredly
have been spared a claimant strong enough to hold
the country in the grasp of civil war till 1208 and
then, profiting by Philip's murder, for another decade
until 1218. But the most interesting parallel of all
is provided by the succession of a nine year old boy
to the English throne in 1216. The situation in
which Henry III ascended the throne was weak
beyond comparison, if it is contrasted with the
position of Germany on the death of Henry VI in

[35] Cf. Rosenstock, MIÖG. XLIV (1930), 404, and Mitteis, *Die deutsche Königswahl* (1938), 95.
[36] On the whole question, cf. Rosenstock, *Königshaus*, 70—73.

1197. The baronage which had forced the charter
on John had now a heaven-sent opportunity to
consolidate its recent gains. Yet in 1216 and again
in 1217 the charter was shorn of its most stringent
checks; and the whole minority is a proof that, when
the opportunity of 1135 recurred, there was no
party both desirous and capable of exploiting it.
The ability of government to carry on during the
absence of, and in spite of the financial strain imposed
by Richard I had been an earlier indication of the
same new outlook, of the same new attitude towards
the constitution. But if the English constitution
could stand the strain of Richard's reign and Henry
III's minority, why, we must ask, was Germany,
which had travelled in 1198 as far along the road
towards hereditary succession and primogeniture
as England, overwhelmed by a situation which, if
serious in comparison with France, was ordinary in
comparison with England? Why, in short, did
Henry VI's death lead to something which, by common consent, was near to collapse? If Henry VI's
reign had really marked the high-point which so
many historians have seen in it, it is difficult to see
why it failed to leave a more substantial legacy.
The sense of English development had been the
creation of an administration which could function
without the king, and which did function without
the king when need arose. Was this the essential
difference between Germany in 1198 and England
in 1189 and 1216? Was the Hohenstaufen *ministerialis*[37] a less trusty instrument than the English
" civil servant " ? Was the discipline which, in two
or three generations, weaned the English baronage

[37] For the *ministeriales* and their place in imperial government, cf.
infra II, 110—111, 209—211, 223—224, 230—232, 262—265, 291.

from the attitude of 1135 lacking in twelfth century
Germany ?   Both of these possibilities probably
represent a part of the truth; but it is not necessary,
for our purpose, to answer the question fully or at
all. It is sufficient if we realize that it is a superficial
attitude to attribute decisive importance to the fate
which robbed Germany of Henry VI at the early
age of thirty-two. A strong constitutional structure,
though it would doubtless have suffered temporarily,
could have stood this strain, as the English constitution stood similar strains; and if accidents like the
premature death of Henry VI were really of decisive
significance, the reason must be sought in some
weakness or deficiency in the constitutional situation.
Once again we see that, though a superficial and
partial explanation of the course of German development can be obtained by an exaggeration of minor
causes or of causes which, although important, were
not so very different from those obtaining elsewhere,
a true and realistic approach leads us behind the
immediate and transitory factors to the ultimate
constitutional forces which alone gave significance to
trivial incidents and external influences. Cause and
occasion rarely coincide in the process of historical
growth; and it is essential to see that the occasions
of change and new departure which still assume a
preponderant place in the explanation of German
internal development were only occasions at which
deeper constitutional causes came to the forefront—
were, indeed, only important at all because there
were elements in constitutional life which were
strong enough to exploit the accidents, incidents and
occasions which German history, like all other history,
threw out as tests of constitutional stability.
    What, then, were these crucial elements in con-

stitutional life ?   What were the factors which made
accidents and influences over which Capetians and
Plantagenets triumphed sometimes easily and often
by herculean effort, the occasions for bitter contest
and peremptory and radical demands ?   We have
already enumerated the three factors which still
receive most attention: the duchies, the elective
monarchy, and the usurpation of regalian rights.
Nor can it be doubted that, granted the assumptions
on which the influence and importance of these factors
is based, they provide us with a simple and not
unconvincing explanation of the unique features of
German constitutional development.   The real question is whether the basic assumption which lies at
the root of each argument can be accepted.   The
duchies, it is still commonly maintained, exerted
decisive influence because they were firmly established,
deep-rooted racial unities, as ancient as the monarchy
if not more ancient, independent in many branches
of constitutional life and with a living memory of
still greater independence; fixed, mature and stabilized elements, in short, which either combined to
create a federal state with a monarch at its head or
(if another view is adopted) were loosely subjected
to the yoke of the German kings.   Tied by its relations with these semi-independent states, the
monarchy—to turn to the second factor in the
constitutional situation—was necessarily weak.   The
king ruled by a tacit if not an open alliance with the
dukes.   A duke himself by origin, he was *primus
inter pares*.   His object, it is true, was to raise
himself and his dynasty to a truly royal position
and above all to introduce hereditary succession;
but election was implicit in the constitutional situation, and the strength of the " stem duchies " meant

that the elective principle, which was overcome in England and France, could never be broken in Germany. Elective *ab initio*, the German king was bound by his beginnings; and as an elective king he was—with a few exceptions in the Ottonian period—a weak king. The crown had to be bought by concessions: the magnates, princes, barons, who should have been servants of the monarchy, became, in consequence of their electoral rights, its masters. Thus we come to the third factor in the constitutional situation. A weak king, dependent on the good-will of his electors, had necessarily to give way to their demands for lucrative and power-giving rights. Offices quickly became hereditary, and the crown was even forced to admit the principle that fiefs and offices could not be retained in royal hands for more than a year and a day.[38] In this way the countship, the basic unit of administration, passed out of royal control and became, instead of a centre of local government and the king's means of keeping his finger on provincial life, a centre of particularism and a means of resistance to the monarchy. Strong in their local independence the counts assumed or usurped regalian rights, and so we get the beginning of the process which Frederick II, impotent to change the situation, legitimized by the statutes of 1220 and 1232. The countship, in short, was transformed into the principality, and with this change the Germany which lasted from the fourteenth to the nineteenth century was born.

[38] On this principle—i.e., the principle of *Leihezwang*—the best discussion is to be found in Mitteis, *Lr. u. Sg.*, 685—701, where the essential fact emerges that the *Leihezwang* was not—as has been widely presumed— an ancient and unalterable principle of German constitutional law, but a specific innovation, introduced under the stress of determinable political circumstances in the second half of the twelfth century, and only slowly acquiring a place as an integral part of constitutional law; cf. Kienast, *HZ.* CLVIII (1938), 14, and for further discussion, *infra*, 129.

What and how much of this lucid and at first glance singularly convincing argument is correct? To answer this question—and an answer is an essential preliminary to further progress—we must consider each of the three elements separately. Not much, I think, will be left of the structure when our task of demolition is ended. For in every case, it will be seen, the arguments used and the " facts " postulated ignore what we have already stated to be the essential feature of German constitutional life: its flexible constantly changing character, its ebb and flow, its lack of rigid immutable elements, its dynamic energy. At the very beginning of German history fixed institutions are postulated, duchies and countships, which, existing unchanged and unchangeable for centuries, moulded the forms of German public life. The German constitution of the middle ages is thus tied, in the case of the countship, to a Carolingian institution, and in the case of the duchy, to a force which is commonly supposed to have sprung, in a remote Germanic past, from the " sub-kingships " of the tribes which settled the German lands. Inevitably we are forced to ask whether the middle ages, so ripe in constructive powers, had nothing to add and nothing to substitute: is development and new creation lacking? Have the German middle ages no institutions which they can call their own? And even if old names—*comitatus, immunitas, advocatia,* and so forth—were retained, was mediaeval Germany so devoid of vital forces that it was unable to give new substance to an ancient organization? Was the organization of public life which we call the constitution something which existed, fixed and immutable, at the beginning of German history, a hard crust which stifled the

vital forces beneath, a rigid superstructure which
not even three centuries of historical growth could
transform ?   Such, we shall see, are the hypotheses
which are still, consciously and unconsciously, maintained; such is the view from which the historians
of a new generation, with a fuller realization of the
constructive energy embodied in mediaeval society,
have broken away.   A brilliant key to the whole
situation has been provided by the remark that " the
strict legality of the mediaeval constitution was the
result, not the precondition of historical evolution."[39]
It is with this observation as our measure that we
must approach the theory of German constitutional
development which has been briefly surveyed.

[39] P. E. Schramm, " Die Krönung in Deutschland bis zum Beginn
des Salischen Hauses," ZRG. *Kanon. Abt.* XXIV (1935), 189; cf. H.
Heimpel, " Bemerkungen z. Geschichte König Heinrichs des Ersten,"
Berichte d. sächsischen Akademie, phil.-hist. Kl. LXXXVIII. iv (1936),
29 n. 4.

II

THE PROBLEM OF THE DUCHIES

NOWHERE is the tendency to presuppose the existence, at the beginning of independent German history, of rigid, mature, well defined institutions more evident than in the theory of the "stem-duchies ".[1] It is not necessary, in this place, to show how illusory is the supposed connexion with the "sub-kingships " of the period of Germanic migration and settlement or even with the duchies of Merovingian and early Carolingian times. By the beginning of the tenth century, even the Mero-

[1] On the "stem-duchies" generally, reference may be made to W. Varges, " Das Herzogtum," *Aus Politik u. Geschichte. Gedächtnisschrift f. Georg v. Below* (1928), 17—31; G. Läwen, *Stammesherzog u. Stammesherzogtum* (1935); H. Heimpel, *Bemerkungen z. Gesch. König Heinrichs des Ersten.* For the older view, cf. particularly W. Sickel, " Das Wesen des Volksherzogtums," HZ. LII (1884), 407—490, and a more moderate account in W. v. Giesebrecht, *Gesch. d. deutschen Kaiserzeit* I (5th ed., 1881), 178—189 (with the notes, pp. 805—806), or A. Hauck, *Kirchengeschichte Deutschlands* III (3rd and 4th ed., 1906), 3—27. For a return to the older view, cf. W. Merk, " Die deutschen Stämme in der Rechtsgeschichte," ZRG. *Germ. Abt.* LVIII (1938), 1—41, with whom, however, I cannot agree, so far as the duchy is at issue. It is true, as Merk insists (p. 38), that the " Stämme " or racial units were not " Traumgebilde einer verstiegenen Stammesromantik, sondern greifbare Wirklichkeit," and in particular that they were the basis of " folk law " (p. 32); but this tells us nothing of the duchy, as distinct from the " stem ". Hauck (p. 5) cautiously concedes that contemporaries might have thought that the " folk " had founded the duchy (" es konnte alsbald die Anschauung entstehen, dass das Volk selbst das Herzogtum gegründet habe "); but he carefully abstains from stating this connexion of folk and duchy as a fact. Merk, on the other hand,—like Sickel—accepts the hypothetical identification of " stem " and duchy as a fact, but without bringing forward evidence to support his view. As will later appear, it seems to me that we must make a sharp distinction between " stem " and duchy, and that the truth about both is obscured by their junction in the conception of a " Stammesherzogtum " or "stem-duchy ". The reality of the " stem " has little connexion with the question of the duchy, and none at all with that of the constitutional position of the duke, whose rights and functions are intangible in the extreme; cf. *infra,* 31, n. 13.—Greater attention is given to the constitutional aspects of the question in E. Klebel, " Herzogtümer u. Marken bis 900," *Deutsches Archiv f. Gesch. d. Mittelalters* II (1938), 1—53.

vingian period was a dim and legendary past, and the realities were very different. It is easy to see the rise of the duchies at the end of the ninth century as " the instinctive and spontaneous rally of the German people, owing to the stress of the time, around their natural and historical tribal representatives ".[2] But the fact remains that the leaders who arose with the decline of Carolingian rule were no more " natural and historical tribal representatives" in Germany than they were in France or Italy.[3] And the duchies themselves, in 911 or 918, were not, and never were to be, solid blocks, formed, stabilized units.[4] Important political factors though they were at the time when Henry I succeeded to the Frankish

[2] J. W. Thompson, *Feudal Germany* (1928), 294.
[3] For Italy, cf. A. Hofmeister, " Markgrafen u. Markgrafschaften im italischen Königreich," MIÖG. *Erg.-Bd.* VII (1907), 215—435, and S. Pivano, *Stato e Chiesa da Berengario I ad Arduino* (1908), 114—150. For France, cf. Guilhiermoz, *Essai sur l'origine de la noblesse en France* (1902), or the facts regarding the rise of counts and viscounts to territorial predominance in Longnon, *La formation de l'unité française* (1922), 41—46. Reynaud sums up the position in France when he says of the dukes, that " ils n'avaient plus au XIe siècle leur caractère ancien. C'était des féodaux commes les autres qui avaient su, à force d'énergie et d'intelligence, imposer leur suzeraineté à un certain nombre de petits comtes ou barons, en dehors de toute espèce de considérations ethnographiques " (p. 35). But were the German dukes any different ? Reynaud admits (p. 118) that " l'ancienne noblesse germanique ayant disparu pendant la période des invasions, ce furent en général des fonctionnaires carolingiens qui se haussèrent à la dignité ducale; " but he still concludes that the German movement was tribal or national, speaks of the duke as " produit indigène " (p. 122) or " chef provincial " (p. 117), and contrasts the position in Germany, where there was a return to a popular " sub-national " duchy, with that in France, where greater " désagrégation " led to a true feudalism (p. 121). But we can admit a difference in the degree to which anarchy fractured local government—a difference the importance of which it is certainly not my wish to minimise—without regarding the German duke as substantially different from his contemporary in late Carolingian France: i.e., the most successful and powerful among the comital families. In this regard, it seems to me, the contrast between France and Germany has been pushed to dangerous extremes.
[4] Cf. Mayer, *infra* II, 8—9, and Rörig, *Partikularismus*, 7: " Ebenso verfehlt ist es aber . . . sich das ostfränkische Reich als Aneinanderreihung einer Zahl von geschlossenen Stammesherzogtümern vorzustellen, wobei . . . zu bemerken ist, wie wenig diese Stämme etwas ein für allemal Fertiges, sondern immer noch in Bewegung Befindliches waren." The position is stated at length and the point conceded by Merk, 3—9.

throne, it was still an open question whether they were going to develop into fixed territorial and administrative units, whether the ducal office was going to become a permanent institution in German constitutional law and organization. It is often forgotten that the title *dux* only gradually received official recognition: from the point of view of the crown, the men whom chroniclers like Widukind and Regino were wont to call *duces*, " leaders ", " military commanders ",[5] were still under Henry I only *comites*, and the term *dux* is rare, as a technical, constitutional appellation, before the reigns of Otto II and Otto III.[6] If the term *dux* goes back in origin to the remote days of the late Roman empire,[7] the specific type of duchy which was struggling into existence when the Saxon dynasty took over rule in Germany was a very recent growth which sprang up in the days of Arnulf (887—899) or Louis the Child (899—911).[8] And its roots were military, not

[5] Varges (p. 30) rightly points out that the title is used indiscriminately by annalists and chroniclers, for whom it has obviously no precise or technical meaning; similarly Läwen, 21, and more generally, pp. 11—13, 30, 34.

[6] Varges, 29—30. Cf. Läwen, 24—25, where it is pointed out that in a charter of 903 only two sorts of prince, bishop and count, are recognized (also p. 18: no recognition of the title " duke of Lotharingia " by the chancery).

[7] Cf. Varges, 18 sqq. But the Latin term *dux* and the German term *Herzog* are, of course, not necessarily identical (Varges, 17), and H. Zeiss, " Herzogsname u. Herzogsamt," *Wiener Prähist. Zeitschr.* XIX (1932), 145—160, argues convincingly that the term *Herzog*—" eine Schöpfung der merovingischen Amtssprache " (p. 160)—and the office which that term implies, cannot be traced back beyond the time of Clovis (p. 155). Cf. also Klebel, 14, who seeks, however, to compromise between Zeiss' and Sickel's views (p. 9).

[8] For the facts, cf. Giesebrecht, *loc. cit.*—There had been a similar movement towards local independence and the usurpation of royal rights under the Merovingians, but it had been broken by Charles Martel and Charlemagne (Varges, 22—23), and Sickel himself admits (p. 408) that there was " no continuity " between the Merovingian and the later German duchies. If he lays no weight on this fact, it is because he sees in the duchy, wherever it emerges and in whatever circumstances, a revival of the idea of a primitive pre-Frankish popular monarchy (p. 140), and this idea, it appears, is for him a sufficient connecting link with the past. But the

tribal or racial.[9]   The Liudolfinger began under
Louis the German (840—876) as *duces orientalis
Saxoniae*—that is to say, as commanders of the
" fyrd " of Eastern Saxony—and not until about
897 does the *ducatus* become hereditary and the
attempt begin to transform a military command
in one part of the Saxon lands into a hegemony
over the Saxon land as a whole.[10]   In Bavaria also
the ducal family sprang from Liutpold, the military
commander in the marks of Carinthia and Bohemia,
whose son Arnulf (907—937) assumed the title of
duke of Bavaria.   Under Louis the Child and Conrad I there were, in short, a few families which, profiting by the disintegration of the times, were creating
for themselves a specially exalted position which
they were calling " ducal " to distinguish it from
that of lesser magnates; but whether this *de facto*
development would be consolidated into a *de iure*
position to which fixed constitutional rights were
attached, whether the duchy would become an
accepted element in the constitution, was a question
which only the history of the tenth century could
decide.   In 918 the duchy was merely the product
of half-a-century of political strife; and fifty years
were not enough to create and define a permanent
institution.[11]   The situation was full of potentialities;

belief that the duchy originated in the primitive monarchy of the Germanic
tribes will not stand the criticism of Varges and Zeiss; and even if it would,
it would still be necessary to prove—with Sickel it is simply a dogma—
that such a conception of the ducal office remained alive at the end of the
ninth century.

  [9] Varges, 23—24; Läwen, 11—13, 30, 34 (" the title in no way expresses a claim to leadership of the race or even to a specific territorial
dominion ").

  [10] Varges, 24 (with evidence for Bavaria also).   Läwen, 17, points
out that the beginning in Swabia also is the military title, *dux Raetiarum*.

  [11] The view taken here is, therefore, exactly contrary to that of
Sickel, who writes (p. 107): " es war nicht ein thatsächliches Machtver-
hältnis und daher ein vorübergehender Zustand, sondern es war eine
verfassungsmässige Ordnung, ein durch das Recht bestimmtes öffentliches

but what had been done under Louis and Conrad
might still be undone, it was not so firmly established
and well-defined that it had necessarily to be accepted.[12] Nor was the lack of official recognition,
which we have already mentioned, a mere formality.
Few, if any, definite rights were as yet attached to
the ducal office.[13] Above all, there was in 918 no

Leben." But Giesebrecht had already implicitly rejected Sickel's view,
when he described the duke's power as "revolutionary"—"eine revolu-
tionäre Gewalt, die nur in dem Drang der Zeitumstände ihre Berechtigung
fand" (I, 806).

[12] Reynaud, 122, also points out that, whereas France suffered some
two centuries of anarchy and disorder, "ils ne s'étendirent guère, chez
nos voisins, que sur une courte période d'une vingtaine d'années." "La
réaction nationale allemande n'aboutit pas, comme la réaction nationale
de notre pays, à l'établissement d'une véritable féodalité. Elle n'en eut
pas le temps."

[13] Current opinion, as reflected, e.g., by Schröder-v. Künssberg,
Lehrbuch d. deutschen Rechtsgesch. (7th ed., 1931), 603, and by v. Schwerin,
Grundzüge d. deutschen Rechtsgesch. (1934), 159, takes a contrary view,
and—besides the leadership of the provincial fyrd—attributes to the dukes
as a minimum the right to hold provincial assemblies and a jurisdiction
superior to that of the counts. But the vagueness of formulation is noteworthy—Schröder, for example, credits the duke with "mehr oder weniger
eine obergerichtliche Tätigkeit," and Waitz (Verf.-gesch. VIII, 44) speaks
of a "gewisse allgemeine Gerichtsbarkeit"—and it is hard to discover the
evidence on which even this indefinite attribution is made. Sickel (p.
426) frankly adopts an a priori attitude: "wenn wir das Wesen des
Herzogtums dahin bestimmen," he writes, "dass es ein volksthümlicher
Unterstaat war, so hat der Herzog, weil er Unterkönig ist, Amtshoheit,
er besitzt Heerhoheit und Gerichtshoheit." But this is at best deduction,
and—although Sickel's point of view seems to have been adopted, at least
unconsciously, by a majority of subsequent historians—it will not stand
confrontation with the facts. It is Läwen's merit to have examined the
supposed ducal functions one by one in the light of the actual evidence.
The evidence for ducal judicial authority, he concludes (p. 42), is very
weak, and applies best to Bavaria alone (p. 36). There is no evidence that
the duke has a constitutional right to summon the tribal assembly, or
that it is "suum placitum" (p. 72), although there is a "Versuch, einen
herzoglichen Hoftag zu konstituieren" (p. 71). Control of county organisation is certainly exercised, but not in a ducal capacity (p. 37), and it is
no monopoly of the dukes. Sickel himself (p. 454) had already conceded
that the duke as such could claim no authority over the church within
his duchy. Apart from the original function of military leadership, therefore, Läwen sees the maintenance of peace, and therefore the control of
the Landfrieden, as the only specifically ducal right (p. 42); but I find it
hard to accept this view (cf. infra, 44). Sickel writes (p. 455): "wir haben
wenigstens die etwaigen Bedenken, ob dem Herzog überhaupt ausgedehnte
Rechte über das Beamtentum zugestanden, hinweg zu räumen"; but, as
he does not fulfil his promise, we are left, so far as I can see, with a de facto
prominence, which might in certain cases amount to predominance, among
the counts, and an occasional function of military leadership in time of

ducal right, and not even a tribal right, to elect the king.[14]   It has long been recognized that Henry I was not elected by the five German peoples, Franks, Saxons, Bavarians, Swabians and Lotharingians;[15] but it is now clear that not even the election by Franks and Saxons alone, which is usually supposed to have created Henry's rights, can be accepted as a historical fact.   Henry, who had been nominated as successor by Conrad I, was " designated ", was introduced to the assembly of Franks and Saxons as king, by the Frankish leader, Eberhard.[16]   " Designation " is the essence of the situation; and designation looms so large precisely because the duchies had not reached a stage of development which would allow them, as juristic personalities represented by their leaders, to undertake the function of election.

The German monarchy, therefore, though it had necessarily to cope with certain definite political tendencies and to prevent their growth, was not faced at the beginning of its history by a firmly rooted, exactly defined institution which was so integral a part of the constitutional order that it formed an insuperable block in the path of monar-

war.   When v. Schwerin concludes: " Die Stellung der Stammesherzöge ruhte mehr auf politischer Macht als auf rechtlicher Befugnis," the only point, therefore, is whether there can be any question of " rechtliche Befugnis " at all, or whether " politische Macht " does not give the whole answer.   And this point is reinforced by the consideration that there is no need to suppose that the geographical and ethnological unit which it is convenient to call the " stem " must have crystallized into an administrative unit represented by the duke.   The relations of duke and folk are obscure and difficult; but it is hard to see that the former represented the latter, and therefore wide of the mark to suppose, as Sickel supposed, that rights accrued to him as representative of a political body.   " Stamm " and " Stammesherzog " cannot, in short, be identified; cf. Mitteis, *Die deutsche Königswahl* (1938), 83—84.

[14] Cf. particularly Heimpel, *Bemerkungen*, where the older literature is summarized and criticised.

[15] Cf. for example Rosenstock, *Königshaus*, 94—96, and Joachimsen, *infra* II, 97.

[16] Heimpel, 27—31.

chical development. " At the accession of Henry I ",
it has been said, " there were neither territorial
duchies nor tribal duchies in Germany. The country
was not an agglomeration of five provinces which
the Saxon rulers welded together into a unity. It
is true, however, that in each of the great regions
certain families had used their power and wealth to
raise themselves above their fellows and, as occupants
of the *ducatus*, were exercising certain rights over the
other lay and ecclesiastical magnates. The *duces*
were introducing themselves, as a new order, between
the king and the counts and margraves."[17]   If this
process, which had begun so vigorously, were carried
to a logical conclusion, the duchy would undoubtedly
become—what it as yet was not—a permanent and
immutable element in the constitution. The decisive
question was whether it would claim and exercise
definite constitutional rights, whether, in matters of
organization and administration, the monarchy would
be forced, by the development of an irrevocable
practice, to work through, and therefore ultimately
in dependence on, the dukes. What, in short, were
the rights which the new ducal families were exercising
over the lay and ecclesiastical magnates of their
districts ?   Were they, in fact, rights or were they
merely powers ?   Long and undisputed exercise
would certainly transform powers into inalienable
rights; but the essence of the situation was that
long and undisputed exercise was nowhere conceded.

[17] Varges, 27—28.   Cf. also p. 24: " Von einem geschlossenen Herr-
schaftsgebiet der Liudolfinger ist keine Rede.   Es ist eine falsche . . . An-
nahme unserer Geschichtswerke, dass Otto und Heinrich die Herren von
ganz Sachsen und Thüringen gewesen seien.   Es gab kein Stammes- oder
Landesherzogtum Sachsen, ebensowenig wie solche Gebilde in Bayern,
Schwaben, Lothringen, Franken vorhanden gewesen sind . . . Das Königtum war nicht so schwach, um solche Gebilde zu dulden, zumal es eine
feste Stütze an der Kirche fand, die die Einheit des Reiches verteidigte
und alle provinziellen Bildungen bekämpfte."

At the crucial moment the Saxon monarchy intervened and the development which had begun at
the end of the ninth century was held up. Ducal
power was built up on the prerogatives which fell
to a leader who could defend his land,[18] and the
decisive factor, it has been acutely suggested,[19] was
the failure of the dukes, of the military leaders in
the various regions, to perform their first duty, the
defeat of the Hungarian invaders: by taking over
and successfully accomplishing this function Henry I
and Otto I definitely established their superiority
and won the initial advantage which enabled them
to stand up against the growing ducal authority and
win back rights which under the later Carolingians
had already passed into ducal hands.[20]   Was the
royal demesne going to be administered and controlled in each particular region by the duke ?   Were
the counts to become dependent, not directly on the
crown, but on the duke in the first place, and only
on the crown through a ducal intermediary ?   Was
the duke to control the churches of his land, to close
them to royal influence, and to centre ecclesiastical
organization, like the county organization, round his
own person ?   These were the three questions to
which a positive answer would make the ducal power
a constitutional as well as a political reality.   We

[18] Läwen, 12—13; Varges, 24.

[19] Rörig, 5.

[20] The general constitutional significance of the invasions of Hun-
garians, Saracens and Northmen throughout Europe is well known—cf.
for example Reynaud, 18 sqq.—although it has never been analysed in
detail.   The East-Frankish Carolingians left defence to the *duces*, and with
this duty went the means and resources wherewith to organize defence.
This renunciation by the monarchy begins the rise of the duchies, just as
the same set of circumstances leads in Italy to the growth of episcopal
predominance; for a comparison, cf. Pivano, 65—67.   After 852 a visit
to Saxony by East-Frankish kings is a rarity, and rights fall to him who
can organize defence; Seidlmayer, *Deutscher Nord u. Süd im Hochmittelalter*
(1928), 26.—Under Henry I and Otto I the process is the very opposite.

cannot attempt to consider them in detail or to trace
the long historical process through which an answer
was sought. The fact is that no definite solution
was achieved until the duchy had sunk in importance
and been obliterated in the later middle ages by the
territorial principality; and the territorial principality, we shall see,[21] was not the immediate successor
of the duchy, it had other roots and represented
other tendencies, its basis was feudal rather than
racial or tribal. To say, as is sometimes maintained,
that the " stem-duchy ", though failing in its immediate objects, decided the fate of Germany by
handing on an inheritance of particularism to the
principalities, is therefore wrong; for the principalities owed their main impetus to tendencies which
emerged in the period of the Investiture Contest,
and the problem of the " stem-duchy "—the problem,
it must be reiterated, whether the " stem-duchies "
were going to establish themselves as fixed elements
in the constitution, and not the problem of dealing
with already existing unities—was already solved
or eliminated by the end of the Ottonian period.

It is well known that the problem of the duchies
is the key to the policy, both internal and external,[22]
of Henry I and Otto I. In this respect there was no
difference between the two rulers. Instead of the
contrast which has so often been expressed in the
saying that Henry relied on the dukes against the
church, Otto on the church against the dukes, their

[21] *Infra*, cap. IV. and cap. V.

[22] For the influence of ducal policy on the Italian and Burgundian
policy of the crown, cf. A. Hofmeister, *Deutschland u. Burgund im früheren
Mittelalter* (1914), M. Lintzel, " Heinrich I u. das Herzogtum Schwaben,"
Hist. Vierteljahrschr. XXIV (1929), 1—17, Heimpel, *op. cit.*, 44—45,
Schmeidler, *infra* II, 75—77.—It is hoped that it will be possible to devote a
subsequent volume of this series to the Empire and imperial and Italian
policy, and a more detailed examination of this aspect of the question is
therefore reserved for that occasion.

policy represents a remarkably consistent whole. Each was concerned to incorporate the new force, which was still without a fixed place in the constitution,[23] into the organization of the realm,[24] and by this incorporation or recognition to check, control and subjugate it: each used, predominantly if not solely, the most effective instrument for realizing this policy: the church. In this regard too much emphasis has been laid on Henry's refusal of anointment as a key to the policy of his reign.[25] Without doubt, the Saxon ruler, who had seen ecclesiastical influence predominant under Conrad and had a lively recollection of the weighty synod of Hohenaltheim in 916,[26] was determined to be no mere nominee of the church; but his refusal to be used by the church did not imply a refusal to use the church. On this point the facts are eloquent.[27] Henry's first care was Swabia, because Swabia, through its close connexion with Burgundy, Italy and the old Middle Kingdom generally, was most likely to endanger the position of the German king and to break up the unity of the German people, of the *regnum Teutonicorum*, which was already a historical fact.[28] By 920 he

[23] " In dem üblichen Schema der karolingischen Ämterverfassung," says Läwen (p. 25), "fand es zunächst keinen Platz;" and later it remained a fact, "dass es eine klare, für alle Herzogtümer gültige Zuständigkeitsverteilung nicht gab " (p. 34).

[24] Heimpel, 29—30.

[25] Heimpel, 37—38, seems to exaggerate both the contrast between Conrad and Henry, and that between Henry and Otto. The essential point is made by Stutz, *Der Erzbischof v. Mainz u. die deutsche Königswahl* (1910), 7—that anointment was refused because Henry "wished above all to avoid the impression that his monarchy owed its establishment to any living person." His refusal, in short, was a symbol of independence, not of hostility to the church.

[26] Cf. Hefele-Leclercq, *Histoire des conciles* IV. ii (1911), 744—749; Hauck, *Kirchengesch.* III, 13—15.

[27] For the following, cf. Lintzel, *Heinrich I. u. d. Herzogtum Schwaben.*

[28] As regards the *regnum Teutonicorum*, cf. *infra*, 49. The whole of Sickel's argument depends, on the contrary, on the supposition that there was still no German people. It is to this period—the " Zeit des Staates ohne Volk "—that the duchies belong; cf. Sickel, 435.

was in control of the royal demesne in Swabia.[29]
But the essential point was whether he would be
able to break the dependence of the Swabian church
on duke Burchard. At the synod which Henry
summoned to Coblenz in 922 only one Swabian pre-
late was present, and it is characteristic that he was
the bishop of Strassburg, the ecclesiastic most
distant of all from Burchard's centre of power.[30]
To break down this isolation of the Swabian church
was the main task of royal policy; but no substantial
progress was possible before Burchard's death in 926.
Henry's appointment of the Frankish Hermann as
Burchard's successor, however, was a decisive step,
as well as an indication that tribal rights, in electing
the duke as in other things, were not so deeply-rooted
as is usually supposed.[31] The new duke was a
" foreigner "; he was nominated by the crown
instead of being designated by a Swabian assembly;
he was an " official "—at any rate by comparison
with Burchard[32]—a representative and agent of the
monarchy.[33] It is characteristic that immediately
after Hermann's appointment royal charters began
to be issued for the Swabian church, Swabian bishops
began to attend the general German synods. In
Swabia, in short, the struggle over ducal power was

[29] Lintzel, 3.
[30] Lintzel, 4.
[31] Lintzel, 8—9, suggests that Hermann's appointment was " funda-
mentally different " from any which had gone before, and that " more
was at stake than a change of person." Succession, he says, had hitherto
been a " matter purely for the ' stem '," and Hermann's appointment by
the crown was therefore a revolutionary step. But this view is not supported
by Läwen, who shows (p. 26) that there is no proof that the duke was or-
dinarily elected by the " folk " (cf. also pp. 62, 63): on the contrary, election was merely an expedient adopted by usurpers who had failed to obtain
royal nomination (Läwen, 65, Sickel, 482).
[32] Haller, HZ. CLIV, 343, rightly insists that the " official " character
of the dukes appointed by Henry I and Otto I must not be exaggerated.
The difference from earlier times, he maintains, " bestand eigentlich nur
im Verzicht auf die Kirchenhoheit, was freilich allein genug bedeutete."
[33] Lintzel, 9.

decided by 926: by recognizing the new element
Henry had, on the one hand, set definite limits to
its competence, had reaffirmed the direct connexion
of crown and church, and on the other hand, the new
duke was a royal nominee, closely bound to the
monarchy.

We cannot stop to trace the detail of the historical
process which had begun in this way. What Henry,
for reasons of expediency, had started in Swabia,
Otto continued in Bavaria. As Henry had recovered
the royal demesne in Swabia, so Otto reasserted control over the Bavarian crown lands.[34]   But already
at the coronation of Otto I in 936 the monarchy's
method of dealing with the new political force had
received striking symbolic expression.   The dukes
not only bound themselves to the monarchy by ties
of vassalage and thus gave the king a handle by which
to reduce them to dependence on the crown, but
they also performed the ceremonial services at the
coronation feast, recognizing in this way their position
as royal servants.[35]   How effective these ties were
was seen only two years later when Arnulf's son,
Eberhard, was deposed because he refused to obey
the royal summons to court.[36]   Otto I's coronation,
therefore, marks a new relationship between dukes
and monarchy, and it has been well said that the
essential precondition of the new situation was
Henry I's policy, which had given the dukes a
definite position in the state and so made it necessary
to include their recognition of the sovereign as a
special act in the coronation ceremony.[37]   But this

[34] M. Spindler, *Die Anfänge des bayerischen Landesfürstentums* (1937), 4
[35] Cf. among many, Schramm, *Krönung in Deutschland*, 208; Rosenstock, 18, 63; Sickel, 466; and *infra* II, 98 and 238 (n. 17).
[36] Sickel, 485.
[37] Heimpel, 29.

recognition of the dukes, which was admittedly a compromise, a first step in the process which was to lead to their subjugation,[38] was in no way a recognition of all, or even of any, of their legal and constitutional claims. The question of their competence was still unsolved: the dukes were still without explicit rights and functions, except perhaps for the duty of military leadership.[39] The attempt to create a ducal hegemony over the provincial churches was definitely broken when the Bavarian church was freed from ducal control in 976. Ecclesiastical organization broke away from ducal organization and the policy of creating a new racial and territorial unit with the aid of the church had failed—indeed, the church was now consciously used to break up any incipient movement towards unification through racial cohesion. The attempt to reorganize state organization on the basis of the duchy, on the other hand, was even less redoubtable. There is no indication at all that the dukes possessed rights of jurisdiction, that they took a place in the judicial hierarchy as intermediaries between king and counts.[40] Nor is there any evidence of wide-reaching administrative control of the county organization. Like many other powerful lords the dukes often held a number of counties which they administered through viscounts[41]—indeed, it is clear that, besides the military root, the claim to a ducal position might

[38] Sickel, 470, 485, 488.

[39] This was still the significance of the terms *dux, ducatus*, as late as the eleventh century; Läwen, 30.

[40] Läwen, 36—37, 42, and finally 80: " das alte Stammesherzogtum war weder wesentlich eine Gerichtsherrschaft, noch waren in ihm Ansätze vorhanden, eine solche zu werden."—Cf. however, Klebel, 12—13, who concludes from the fact that Otfried (writing *c.* 870) describes Pilate as " herizoho ", that the duke was a " high-placed judge ". The conclusion, unsupported as Klebel admits it to be by direct evidence, seems forced.

[41] Läwen, 37.

sometimes be based on a predominant position among the counts.[42]   The families which called themselves dukes in Swabia and Franconia, for example, were simply the holders of the largest agglomeration of counties.[43]   None of the ducal families, however, obtained constitutional rights over the whole network of counties within their region. Even in Bavaria, which has long been regarded as an exceptionally strong centre of ducal power, it is now an accepted fact that the majority of counts were directly dependent on the crown and free from intermediate ducal control.[44]   This is a very significant fact. Success in this direction would have safely anchored the duchy into the constitution:[45] failure definitely meant that the ducal houses had been unable to transform their power into a position of acknowledged constitutional right. If we seek rights and functions which were specifically ducal, we shall not find them. The dukes had secured personal recognition, but the duchy, as a potential administrative unit, had failed to obtain a fixed place in the constitution and in governmental organization.

The historical development, therefore, which at the end of the ninth century produced outstanding families who expressed their predominance by

[42] *Ibid.*, 53.

[43] Giesebrecht, 183–4; Läwen, 15, 23.

[44] Cf. Spindler, 122, who follows Doeberl, *Entwicklungsgesch. Bayerns* I (1916), 171. Läwen, 39, 57, and Mitteis (*infra* II, 275) maintain the contrary theory, as put forward by Ficker-Puntschart (*Vom Reichsfürstenstande* II. iii).—It is only in regard to Bavaria that the question arises.

[45] Läwen implies as much, p. 39.—Klebel, 49, states that the tenth-century duchy, with certain exceptions, developed "dadurch, dass der vorhandene *dux* oder *marchio* das Ernennungsrecht über die Grafen . . . an sich zog." That this was the tendency of the times, is no doubt true; but Klebel has not proved that the tendency was effective. The evidence of direct relations between crown and counts indicates that the autonomy with which Klebel credits the dukes and margraves remained an unfulfilled aspiration.

calling themselves dukes, never received legal recognition and definition.[46] It was not a strong
enough movement to impose itself, simply because
it was a purely political movement which reflected
the rise of powerful men to powerful positions, but
never ceased to be based on power alone. The
association of the " stem ", the " folk ", with the
ducal house, if it ever occurred, was too transitory
to create a new institution. We have seen how easily
the claim—if such a claim was ever conceived—to
have a native duke, chosen by the people, was dis-
missed in Swabia in 926; and this case is typical
rather than exceptional. Election and hereditary
succession are both in the air in the early decades
of the tenth century, but they never materialize.[47]
And they fail to substantiate because, as SICKEL
himself admits,[48] the " folk " never won a position
in which it could claim the right to elect or to be
ruled by a hereditary line: the loose racial unit,
in short, never became a constitutional unit. The
well-known policy of intervention, division, transference and abolition, which becomes so marked as
the tenth century proceeds, was therefore not a
policy directed to the destruction of an already
existing institution, but a policy which sought to
prevent the transformation of the powers exercised
by certain houses into constitutional rights and their
junction with a certain racial cohesion and independence which existed as a fact without being of constitutional importance.

And this policy was successful. The facts are
well known and only a few illustrations are neces-

[46] Läwen, 52: the duke's position, he says, " ging . . . aus einer jurist-
isch nie klar gefassten historischen Entwicklung hervor."
[47] Läwen, 25—26, 62—65.
[48] *Op. cit.*, 486.

sary.[49]   Bavaria, says SICKEL,[50] was treated like a geographical expression, which could be divided at will; the Saxon duchy came to an end in 918—for the duchy vested in the Billunger family was simply a title conferred by the crown to denote military leadership in the Saxon marches, and carried with it no powers over the Saxon people[51]—and a separate duchy of Franconia ceased to exist in 939;[52] Henry III retained Bavaria in his hands until 1042, Swabia until 1045, Carinthia until 1057.   Between 995 and 1096, it has been calculated, Bavaria remained for thirty-five years in the hands of the king, his son or his consort.   Henry III conferred it seven times in seventeen years, twice to a child and once to a woman, and between 947 and 1180 it saw four Saxon, five Swabian and seven Frankish dukes, while the dukes of Swabia between 926 and 1080 included ten Franks, two Saxons and only one Swabian.[53]

The policy which the Saxon and Salian emperors pursued has been criticized because it assumed that the question was one of persons and not of institutions, and an attack on persons could never shake the foundations of an established institution.[54]   But the essential flaw in this criticism is the fact that the tenth-century duchy, as we have seen, lacked all the attributes of an institution.   Precisely because it

[49] Cf. Varges, 29.

[50] *Op. cit.*, 486.

[51] This fact, firmly established in 1863 by Steindorff, *De ducatus qui Billingorum dicitur origine et progressu*, has once again been emphasized, in view of current misconceptions, by Haller, HZ. CLIV, 343.   Cf. in general R. Hildebrand, *Der sächsische " Staat" Heinrichs des Löwen* (1937), 11.

[52] Cf. Schmeidler, *infra* II, 81 sqq., where the gradual separation of the Nordgau from Bavaria is also explained.   The transformation of Franconia by the addition of its central and upper provinces (II, 84) is an apt illustration of the looseness of racial divisions.

[53] Sickel, 485.

[54] Läwen, 82—83.

was no institution but simply the expression of the political predominance of certain families, the methods adopted by the monarchy were adequate and successful. The duchy had rearisen, at the end of the ninth century, as a title usurped by a few powerful men to mark their preeminence, and it sank back, after a period in which it seemed as though it really might receive constitutional content, into a mere title. This fact is aptly illustrated by the titular duchy of Zähringen, which was created in the last decade of the eleventh century.[55] The creation, like the usurpation of the ducal title two centuries previously, marked the family as outstanding, was a tribute to its power and distinction; but that it expressed any definite legal rights or a specific constitutional position is clearly untrue.[56] Otto of Freising's statement that the duchy was "an empty title" is to be taken literally. On the other hand, the history of the dukes of Zähringen is, as MAYER has shown, a convincing proof that the old title could receive a new meaning and a real significance. This is, in fact, precisely what occurred throughout Germany in the twelfth century. But the mere survival of the name from one age to another does not imply the survival of an institution. The twelfth century duchies have no connexion with what the tenth century dukes tried to be but never succeeded in being. Much has been made of the supposedly

[55] Cf. Th. Mayer, *infra* II, 175—202. The actual cause of the creation was to settle the Swabian question. Bertold of Zähringen had been put forward as duke of Swabia by the anti-king, Rudolf of Rheinfelden; and he was allowed to keep the ducal title as a compromise, on his surrender of this ineffective claim.

[56] This statement is not intended as a denial of the particular constitutional significance—namely, a claim to "autonomy" or to equality with any other provincial power—which Mayer (p. 193) attributes to the title; but there are, I think, good grounds for attributing this meaning to the new developments which, as we shall see, created a new type of duchy in the twelfth century.

ducal function of preserving and maintaining public peace: his leadership in the *Landfrieden* movement, his part in propagating the idea of *treuga terrae,* is supposed to have been not only the main function of the duke, or even the only specifically ducal function, but also the connecting link between the old " stem-duke " and the new ducal powers of the twelfth century.[57]   But the evidence is very incomplete and unconvincing.[58]   There is, indeed, a marked difference from France and England, where the " peace movement " of the eleventh and twelfth centuries played directly into the hands of the king;[59] but in Germany it was the new territorial powers, which might or might not be regarded as ducal—and to the nature of which the appellation in any case made little difference[60]—which led the movement and profited by it.[61]   In any case, it is no longer possible to regard leadership of the " peace movement " as the main root of the new ducal power.   The real source was feudal overlordship over counties and hundreds.[62]   Both Adam of Bremen and Giselbert of Mons, in statements of the highest constitutional importance,[63] describe the duchy as

[57] Läwen, 42—51, following Rosenstock (*Herzogsgewalt u. Friedens-schutz,* 1910) and Hirsch (*Hohe Gerichtsbarkeit,* 204 sqq.)

[58] Läwen admits as much, when he concedes (p. 49) "dass im 12. Jahrhundert der Stamm nicht mehr allein der Träger einer landschaftlich-en lokalen Institution sein konnte.   Die Ablösung des Stammes, des Personalverbandes, durch das Dominium, die neue territoriale Kategorie, war schon zu weit fortgeschritten."   And Sickel before him had been forced (pp. 446–7) to a similar admission.

[59] Hirsch, HG. 237; cf. particularly J. Goebel, *Felony and Misdemeanour* I (1937).

[60] With regard (for example) to Bavaria, cf. Spindler, 173–4, 178.

[61] What is maintained here, therefore, is the old view established by Herzberg-Fränkel, " Die ältesten Land- u. Gottesfrieden in Deutschland," *Forsch. z. deutschen Gesch.* XXIII (1883), 117—163. Läwen himself (p. 49) cites the case of count Robert II of Flanders, who established a peace " per totam terram suam " in 1111.

[62] Mitteis, *infra* II, 270.

[63] Cited by Mitteis, *infra* II, 258 n. 98, and 268 n. 125.

a conglomeration of counties, all feudally dependent on the duke, and their statements are fully borne out by modern investigation.[64] Many of the new duchies—Austria or Würzburg, for example—had no connexion at all with the old tribal divisions; but even where, as in Saxony or Bavaria, the old name remained, boundaries and geographical formation and sometimes even racial composition are essentially different.[65] Henry the Lion's " state " is a duchy of the new feudal and territorial type situated in the lands inhabited by the Saxon people but not comprising the whole of Saxony,[66] and the same is substantially true of the Wittelsbach territory in Bavaria. It is true that the ducal title, where it existed, was maintained as an expression of high dignity and consequently as a useful means of emphasizing sovereign rights and enforcing claims which went beyond the law;[67] but *dux*, in the thirteenth or even in the twelfth century, is simply *dominus terrae*, *ducatus* is *principatus*,[68] and there is no means of distinguishing the dukes from the other members of the new *Reichsfürstenstand* who could claim no inheritance, however illusory or " imaginary ",[69] from a supposedly racial duchy of a remote century.[70]

[64] The basis of all further study is Ficker's classic work, *Vom Reichsfürstenstande* (vol. II, ed. Puntschart, 1911—1923). Cf. further Spindler, 9, 90, 92, 105, 113, and Hildebrand, 103, 110, 177, 185-7, whose whole thesis is contained in the statement (p. 47): " Herzog ist, wer in einem grösseren Territorialgebiet die Summe aller Grafschaften in seiner Hand vereinigt." Whatever other failings the book may have (cf. Hüttebräuker, ZRG. *Germ. Abt.* LVII, 574—586), this thesis seems to me to be proven up to the hilt.—Finally, cf. Mitteis, *infra* II, 267 sqq.

[65] Spindler, 185—186.

[66] Hildebrand, 32.

[67] Spindler, 99, 173, etc.

[68] Cf. Spindler's section, " ' Princeps ' und ' terra '," pp. 169—182.

[69] Spindler, 113.

[70] Rosenstock's attempt (particularly cap. VIII) to prove that the basis of the new " estate of princes " (*Reichsfürstenstand*) of the period after 1180 was, and only could be, an ancient *Stammland* or—and that was the constitutional innovation of the twelfth century—a marcher princi-

For this reason we can leave the twelfth century duchy until we come to speak of the rise of the territorial principalities; it is enough for our present purpose to establish the fact that their history fits in with this new development of a new age, and not, however remotely, with the development of the tribal or racial duchies which failed, because of the revival of the monarchy under the Saxon rulers, to establish themselves as fixed elements in the constitution.

pality, is unconvincing and schematic, and has not won general acceptance. Actual political power and the actual territorial situation, and not a fixed rule of constitutional law, were the decisive factors in determining who should be accounted a member of the new princely class.   Cf. v. Dungern, MIÖG. XXXVII (1917), 499—501, and Kienast, HZ. CLVIII (1938), 9 sqq.

III

THE MONARCHY AND ITS RESOURCES

In attempting to reduce the conception of the " stem-duchy " to its proper place in constitutional history we must be careful not to underestimate its political importance. There is no doubt whatever that the tendency to disintegration into four or five racial divisions and the growing concentration of monar-chical powers in the hands of local leaders was a serious menace to the Saxon rulers and their main preoccupation. It was, without doubt, a source of political weakness and, until it was overcome, a stumbling block in the path of the monarchy and of royal attempts to establish a stronger monarchical power. There is no doubt, further, that the fact of racial disunity—though no more serious than that of tenth century England[1]—favoured the pretensions of provincial magnates. But the pretensions them-selves were political pretensions and could be over-come by political measures: they were due to the weakening of the monarchy in the face of the in-vasions and irruptions of the ninth century and could be overcome by a reassertion of monarchi-cal powers, provided that the monarchical reaction arrived before the new political forces were firmly anchored in the constitution, endowed with rights

[1] A comparison of the position of the German dukes with that of the pre- and post-Conquest earls might prove instructive. Before the twelfth century and the growth of the new forces released by the Investiture Con-test, the position of the German dukes was as indefinite as that of the Anglo-Norman earl, to whom no historian would attribute specific constitutional functions. On the other hand, the potentialities of the position which the earls claimed, but failed to substantiate, become more apparent through a comparison with their peers in Germany.

and recognized as stable elements in the organization of the realm.

And this, at least, was achieved. The Saxon and Salian kings still had redoubtable political opposition to face; but their prompt action saved them from the far more difficult task of uprooting an established institution. Weak as were the foundations which the East Frankish rulers left for the German kings of the Saxon dynasty, they were strong as compared with the basis on which the wielders of ducal power had to build. The inheritance of the dukes goes back to the dark days of the dying ninth century: the inheritance of the German kings reaches back to the heights of the Frankish monarchy. The German monarchy, indeed, is the Frankish monarchy: Henry I, on his elevation to the throne, ceases to be a Saxon and passes under Frankish law,[2] adopts the traditions and takes over the powers of the Frankish kings,[3] becomes a Frank.[4] And this Frankish tradition was not, like so much tradition, an empty shell. It meant at the very least that the German monarchy did not have to start anew in 919 on a new foundation. The proceedings at Forchheim, in which Henry I was accepted as king, implied, as SICKEL has written,[5] the "maintenance of an existing state," the acceptance of the Frankish monarchy. But even more than this was implied. The Frankish kings had welded, however imperfectly, the races they ruled into a unity, and this unity, the *regnum Theutoni-*

[2] Rosenstock, *Königshaus*, 10—11.

[3] *Ibid.*, 18.

[4] Cf. Schramm, *Krönung*, 212, and *infra* II, 82, 98.

[5] " Die in Forchheim Versammelten haben sich über die Fortsetzung des bestehenden Staates geeinigt. Die in der Entstehung begriffenen stammesherzoglichen Gewalten haben nicht nach Befreiung von dem Reich oder nach Beseitigung des Reichs, sondern nach neuen Rechten im Reich gestrebt," *Göttingische Gel. Anzeigen* CLXV (1903), 822, cited by Rörig, 35.

corum, was also maintained intact.[6] The Frankish
kings, with whom Henry I was now associated, were
more than rulers over the Frankish people: their
realm was the *regnum Theutonicorum,* and the unity
of this realm is an undeniable historical fact. It is
characteristic that, at the moment when tribal
separatism is supposed to have been flourishing
unchecked, Arnulf of Bavaria's object was not to
set up a separate Bavarian state—whether duchy
or kingdom is of small importance—but to wrest the
regnum Theutonicorum from Henry.[7] This tacit
acceptance of the Frankish heritage by one of those
whose ducal strivings were threatening to destroy
the work of the Frankish kings is striking testimony
that in 919 more than a mere tradition of a monarchy
over the German peoples survived. Not merely a
nebulous idea of a monarchical overlordship but the
traditional royal authority, by whomsoever it might
be exercised, was accepted by all parties in 919.
" Even if Conrad, Henry and Otto I were kings by
election," it has been said,[8] " the election merely
determined who was to wield the existing royal
authority and was not a reconstitution and confer-
ment of royal authority on the part of supposedly
autogenous tribal powers. That the elected ruler
was legally considered a Frank is a clear indication
that he was taking over existing powers superior
to those of the aristocratic leaders in the various
racial divisions—namely, the authority of the Frankish or East Frankish kings. And the solid basis of
this royal authority was the unity of the lands over
which it was exercised, the fact that the legal conception of an " East Frankish kingdom " corresponded

[6] Rosenstock, *Königshaus,* 7.
[7] Mitteis, *infra* II, 236.
[8] Rörig, 6.

D

to the vital reality of an indivisible German realm."
Only an exaggeration of the stability and permanence
of the tribal divisions, only a mistaken conception of
the fixity and mature organization of the " stem-
duchies " can turn the hard fact of firmly established
royal authority into an empty, almost mythical
tradition of monarchical rule, handed down from
Frankish times. The persons who were calling themselves dukes were, without doubt, the most powerful
force of the age, the mightiest group with which the
king had to deal. " But this patent fact may be
admitted without supposing that, at the beginning
of the tenth century, it was an established legal and
constitutional belief that a king and a kingdom
could only be created by a sort of contract with
the duchies which, in this view, were the real states
at the beginning of German history and could alone
establish a state above themselves. However important the dukes may have been, there still existed,
in the traditions of the church and in Frankish
tradition, a consciousness of the unity of the continental races outside the West Frankish limits.
It is not necessary to exaggerate the Frankish
character of the German kingdom in order to
recognize that—above all, at the moment of
transition from a Frankish to a German kingdom—
the handing over of royal authority by the Frankish
folk was more important than the consent of the
' stem-duchies '."[9]

It is out of the question for us to consider here in
detail either the legal character or the development
of the German monarchy. What we have already
said is a sufficient indication that it was not limited,
at the beginning of its history, by specific organized

[9] Heimpel, 30.

tribal institutions which, if they had existed, would
have placed it in a different and less fortunate position than the monarchy in France or England.   It
is well, also, to see, as the work of HEIMPEL has shown,
that the transference of authority from Frank to
Saxon, the accession of a new dynasty to the Frankish
inheritance, was achieved by a process of " designation " which was the work of the Franks alone, acting
in the person of their leader, Eberhard.[10]   The
change of dynasty, therefore, was not made the
occasion for the assertion of novel electoral principles:
no precedent was created which might have bound
the monarchy in the future, no step was taken which
radically differentiated the German monarchy from
the West Frankish.   It is true that, as time passes,
the contrast between election and hereditary
succession becomes prominent in German history;
but there is nothing specifically German in this antithesis, which is best understood when considered—
as KERN has considered it—in its broad European
setting.   Blood-right, election and consecration were
the primary constituents of royal authority in all
the states of mediaeval Europe.[11]   If in thirteenth
century Germany the electoral element was predominant, this was the result of a long historical
development, and not a permanent fact which had
dominated the German position from the very beginning.   Moreover we must not forget the radical
transformation which the idea of " election " under-

[10] Much the same conclusion had already been formulated by Rosenstock, 94—96.

[11] Cf. F. Kern, *Gottesgnadentum u. Widerstandsrecht* (1914), which
S. B. Chrimes is translating in a later volume in this series under the
title: *Kingship, Law, and Constitution in the Middle Ages*.   Cf. also P. E.
Schramm's innumerable works on the coronation rites, and for Germany
(in addition to Rosenstock), Joachimsen, *infra* II, 97 sqq.

went in this period of three hundred years.[12] " Election " in the tenth century, so far as we can define its content, was never more than " choice " in the broadest sense, and usually no more than " assent ". *Laudatio* or *collaudatio* expresses the meaning of the legal act better than *electio*: " acclamation " is the people's share in the making of its ruler,[13] and " election " in the sense of " choice " or " designation " of his successor normally falls to the reigning king himself. But even if we use the word " election" in a strict mediaeval sense, we shall be wrong if we presuppose an antithesis between election and hereditary right: they are rather two different ways of revealing what is right and what must rightly be, and a third way is added when, with the accession of Otto I, consecration becomes an essential element in the making of a German king. The unity of this threefold revelation of God's will, it has been said, is characteristic of the Ottonian age, its destruction marks the beginning of a new era;[14] but even in the twelfth century, it may be noted, the ideal of a harmonious cooperation of the three elements remains alive and is expressed by Ivo of Chartres.[15]

The " coronation order " which seems to have been composed in Mainz for the elevation of Otto II in 961,[16] and which closely follows the ceremony devised for the coronation of Otto I in 936,[17] is the best

[12] For an illuminating discussion of this subject, cf. P. Schmid, *Der Begriff d. kanon. Wahl in d. Anfängen d. Investiturstreits* (1926).

[13] For acclamation, with particular regard to the army—" nam exercitus facit imperatorem . . . et imperium a solo Deo habetur "—cf. E. E. Stengel, *Hist. Aufsätze Karl Zeumer* (1910), 247 sqq. Cf. Mitteis, *Königswahl*, 106.

[14] Schramm, *Krönung in Deutschland*, 215.

[15] " Si enim rationem consulimus, iure in regem est consecratus, cui iure hereditario regnum competebat, et quem communis consensus episcoporum et procerum iampridem elegerat." Cf. Kern, 100.

[16] Schramm, 223–4.

[17] *Ibid.*, 197.

expression of the tenth century conception of the German monarchy.[18] The terms *electio, eligere*, although they had appeared in the models on which the *ordo* was based, were carefully avoided,[19] and no binding promise was imposed, as in France, on the new king.[20] All the emphasis falls, on the contrary, on hereditary right and on divine right. The king is Christ's vicar, " cuius nomen vicemque gestare crederis ": Christ has appointed him to be " mediator " between clergy and people: his " regnum " is " a Deo concessum ". But God has delegated the throne to his appointed by hereditary right: he holds it by " paternal succession ".[21] And this statement is no theory or courtier's doctrine, but a recognition of existing fact. Otto the Great had gone beyond the old, well-established right of " designating " his successor, and had had his son, Otto II, raised to the throne as co-ruler in 961,[22] and even after Otto I's death in 973 it was from 961 that Otto II's regnal years ran. In the same way Henry III's regnal year began with the death of his father and not with his own coronation.[23] These facts, and still more the minority rule of Otto III and Henry IV[24] and the regencies of royal mothers,[25]

[18] *Ibid.*, 272–4.

[19] Where Widukind's account of Otto I's coronation has the sentence: " si vobis ista electio placeat, dextris in caelum levatis significate," the Mainz *ordo* (§ 8) directs the bishop to ask the *populus*, " si tali principi ac rectori se subicere ipsiusque regnum firma fide stabilire atque iussionibus illius obtemperare velint."

[20] Schramm, 241.

[21] " Sta et retine locum amodo, quem hucusque paterna successione tenuisti, hereditario iure tibi delegatum per auctoritatem Dei omnipotentis et presentem traditionem nostram, omnium scilicet episcoporum ceterorumque Dei servorum " (Schramm, 320).

[22] Schramm, 245.

[23] *Ibid.*, 302.

[24] Perels, *Erbreichsplan*, 57.

[25] On the regency of the empresses, which is not " Sorge für das Kind, sondern Hausgewalt " (Heusler, *Institutionen* II, 453), and which none but the *Hausvorsteher* can exercise, cf. Rosenstock, 31—36, 70—76.

illustrate the firm establishment of the hereditary principle. In the whole period from 911 to 1254 the right of the king's son to succeed, the right of the father to nominate a son as successor, was an accepted axiom of public law;[26] and since election conferred the royal dignity on the whole dynasty and not merely on the single ruler,[27] the succession of a new king from the old line was a matter solely for the royal house to decide and not the business of princes or people.[28] There was, indeed, no question of excluding " election ", for the king who was no despot desired the acclamation and support of his *curia*; but in the circumstances which obtained " election " could only signify assent, affirmation of the royal proposal, in the same way as the *concilium regis* was called on to assent to questions of peace and war and public policy.[29] Rejection of the king's proposal, a demand for reconsideration, is conceivable,[30] but not an " election " in the modern sense of the term, not a " free election ", for the magnates consulted had no alternative to " electing " the king's son.[31]

The situation was, of course, radically different

---

[26] Rosenstock, 39. He rightly points out (p. 41) that even Rudolf of Rheinfelden attests the strength of this principle in 1077, in the very act of abandoning it. And cf. p. 86: " Sogar bei dem Umsturz von 1077, als die Forderung der Sohneswahl statt der Sohnesfolge erhoben wird, gilt es als selbstverständlich, dass Rudolfs Sohn der nächste und wichtigste Thronkandidat sein wird, an dem man nur aus den gewichtigsten Gründen vorbeigeht."

[27] Kern, 18; Rosenstock, 48.

[28] Rosenstock, 51, 62—63, 65—67.

[29] Rosenstock, 40; Schramm, 245.

[30] It seems to have occurred, for example, at the time of Otto I's designation by his father (" Perplures diiudicabant Heinricum regno potiri, quia natus esset in aula regali; alii vero desiderabant Ottonem possidere principatus honorem, quia aetate esset maior et consilio providentior "); but it is characteristic that the old king eventually got his own way—for Liutprand specifically attributes Otto's success to Henry I's personal exertions. Cf. Kern, 32.

[31] Rosenstock, 47.

when there was no direct successor from the royal house, as (for example) after the death of Otto III in 1002. A new royal house had then to be chosen, and it is clear that, in such a situation, there was always the possibility of an *electio libera*.[32] For this reason great emphasis has always been laid on the rapid extinction of the German royal dynasties, on the fate which prevented one long line of rulers consolidating its position, like the Capetian house in France.[33] But the fact is that, for the first two centuries of German history, the so-called " free elections " are the most striking proof of the strength of hereditary principles. Henry II was elected as the successor to the Saxon inheritance: the sole basis of his candidature was his hereditary right.[34] In 1034 the only two candidates who were considered both claimed as descendants of Otto I's daughter, Liutgard, and Conrad II succeeded to no small degree, on the one hand, because of the Carolingian blood in the veins of his wife, Gisela,[35] and on the other, because Henry II's widow, Kunigunde, handed him the royal insignia and thus " designated " him as the candidate best qualified to succeed.[36] Even after the revolutionary storms of the last years of the eleventh century the belief in hereditary right is still a part of the common German inheritance. Lothar III was, in the last analysis, only an anti-king set up in opposition to the legitimate heirs,[37]

[32] On this subject, cf. Rosenstock, cap. V (" Echte Wahlen u. Wechsel des Königshauses ").

[33] *Supra*, 17.

[34] Schramm, 283; Rosenstock, 98.

[35] Rosenstock, 14.

[36] Wipo, *Gesta Conradi*, c. 2 (ed. Bresslau, 1915), p. 19: " Supradicta imperatrix Chunegunda regalia insignia, quae sibi imperator Heinricus reliquerat, gratanter obtulit et ad regnandum, quantum huius sexus auctoritatis est, illum corroboravit." Cf. Schramm, 292.

[37] Cf. Mitteis, *infra* II, 241.

his election was the last of the revolutionary acts which had torn Germany under Henry IV; but even he could emphasize claims of blood,[38] and after his death the traditional attitude was once again predominant. The princes, wrote Sigebert of Gembloux, could not tolerate a king without royal blood in his veins—he was referring to Lothar and Welf—and so they set up Conrad III, a man of royal birth.[39] Far from the extinction of the ruling dynasty being the sign for a consolidation of supposed electoral "rights", nothing is more remarkable than the disinclination to use this opportunity for strengthening particularist claims and princely pretensions. Instead of building up a right of free choice, the princes seem mainly concerned, on such occasions, in genuinely discriminating between the reasonable claims of junior branches of the royal house. It is characteristic that the opportunities for princely egotism which such events as the death of Otto III presented, were allowed to pass if not altogether without exploitation[40] at all events without any direct attempt to weaken the position of the monarchy, and that when a real attempt was made to put electoral principles into play in 1077, it was part of a revolutionary programme. The conception of real "election" arises, in short, not as the result of the lack of direct heirs, not because Germany frequently found itself without an acknowledged successor, but as an explicit breach of tradition in circumstances which were revolutionary. Instead of exploiting

[38] Rosenstock, 88 n. 11, where the conclusions of v. Dungern, *Thronfolgerecht u. Blutsverwandtschaft der deutschen Kaiser* (2nd ed., 1910) are summarized.

[39] "Non ferentes principes Teutonici regni, aliquem extraneum a stirpe regia sibi dominari, regem constituerunt sibi Cunradum, virum regii generis"; cf. Rosenstock, 86.

[40] Cf. for example Schramm, 287–8.

the occasions presented by the death of a childless
king, the princes manufactured an occasion when the
time was ripe.   This fact, which is rarely observed,
is a striking indication that the growth of the electoral principle in Germany is due, not to the under-
mining of hereditary principles by frequent changes
of dynasty, but to the growth of new ideas and of
a new outlook.   It is not our business, at the moment,
to explain or discuss this new atmosphere which
sprang from a novel combination of ancient Germanic
and clerical conceptions of the right to resist constituted authority,[41] and which was, historically, an
answer to the centralizing policy of the Salian kings
with its inevitable hostility to ancient law and
popular custom.[42]   For us the essential fact is to see
the revolutionary nature of the electoral claim
enunciated at Forchheim in 1077.   It was not the
culmination of a gradual process, but a breach of
tradition, a denial of current practice, and an attempt to sever continuity with the past.   In the cleft
were planted the seeds of a new age.

But it has been acutely remarked that the Investiture Contest, though it may have been the
occasion for the definition and consolidation of
clerical and princely claims, was equally the occasion
for a definition and strengthening of monarchical
ideas, that the new emphasis on electoral rights
necessarily produced its reaction, a heightened belief
in the monarchy and in monarchical rights.[43]   We

[41] Professor Kern's volume: *Kingship, Law and Constitution* will deal
with this topic in detail.

[42] " Nihil aliud se postulare, quam . . . ut sua singulis patrimonia per
vim seu per calumniam erepta restituat . . . , ut libertatem genti suae et
legittima a primis temporibus statuta rata atque inviolata manere sinat,"
wrote Lambert of Hersfeld; cf. Kern, *Gottesgnadentum*, 198, and in general
Joachimsen, *infra* II, 110 sqq.

[43] Kern, 236 sqq.

have been warned against regarding the election of
1125 as a final victory for the principle of " free
election ",[44] and JOACHIMSEN has rightly pointed out
that, important as the Investiture Contest was in
German constitutional development, its importance
did not lie in the transference of emphasis from hered-
ity to election: " the view that the German kingdom
was an elective monarchy," he says, " did not
become finally prevalent until some two centuries
after the election of Rudolf of Rheinfelden."[45] It
was only in the thirteenth century—under the stress
of very different circumstances—that election became
the decisive element in the making of a German
king.[46] It is true, indeed, that the old feeling of
stability and solidity is lacking in the twelfth century. PERELS not only points out that, although
succession by primogeniture was possible at all three
elections subsequent to the death of Conrad III in
1152, the eldest son was on no occasion chosen, but
also notes the new emphasis which is placed on the
electoral rights of the princes, for example, in the
Würzburg decrees of 1165.[47] Perhaps it is not far-
fetched to attribute this change of emphasis to
Henry V's break with his father's policy, and his
attempt to cooperate with the nobility.[48] Nevertheless the hereditary principle was adequately safe-
guarded in so far as the new king was, in each case,
taken from the *stirps regia*;[49] and when Henry VI,

[44] Rosenstock, 88.
[45] *Infra* II, 127.
[46] But the double election of 1197 was " a milestone along this road ";
Mitteis, *Königswahl*, 197 (" Bis dahin gibt es gar keine " Königswahl" im
eigentlichen Sinne, es gibt nur in sich zusammenhängende Erhebungsakte
von oft mehrjähriger Dauer, in die die Wahl fest eingegliedert ist ").—
Chapters IV—VI of this book provide the best survey of the growth of
the electoral principle and of the electoral college between 1198 and 1273.
[47] *Der Erbreichsplan Heinrichs VI*, 58, 60—61.
[48] Cf. *infra* II, 156 sq.
[49] Perels, 58.

who, elected in 1167, had been co-regent since 1184 and sole ruler after Barbarossa went on crusade, succeeded in 1190 and dispensed with re-election, the chroniclers were not wrong in maintaining that he followed " quasi successione hereditaria ".[50]

Even after the Investiture Contest, therefore, and in spite of the constitutional transformations of the twelfth century which we have still to consider, the hereditary principle was vigorous and—by 1190—predominant. Before the revolution under Henry IV, on the other hand, there had been no question at all of " election " in the sense in which the term is used to-day. Once again it is worth emphasizing that, under the Ottonian and Salian rulers, blood-right and election were the opposite of antitheses. In West Francia election, oaths, consecration, coronation, investiture and other formalities had been piled together, a mass of uncoordinated forms and acts, with the object of strengthening weak and disputed claims—an agglomeration which was a confession of legal hesitancy and uncertainty, a vain attempt to counter treason and faithlessness. In Germany the same acts and forms, organically combined, were a testimony to a high consciousness of legality and of the strength derived from strict legality. Native Germanic tradition, feudal practice, Christian belief, each demanded consideration, each had its place: because each of the three factors was a constituent element in constitutional life none could be ignored without injury to established right. " With these facts in mind we can understand the juxtaposition, so characteristic of Ottonian times, of factors which were later to become exclusive antitheses. The father's will, the electors' will, God's will; enthrone-

[50] *Ibid.*, 63.

ment by laity and clergy; hereditary right, election, divine right; anointment, spiritual investiture, coronation, the symbolic feast—how many heterogenous traditions are here fused together! How many elements supplement and strengthen each other which after the Investiture Contest will be played off the one against the other! Such fusion is not the result of hesitancy, not incompetence of constitutional thought, but a reflection of the first happy day in German history—the day on which princes, clergy and people joined together under divine guidance in favour of one monarch and the monarch himself asserted unchallenged every right to which a ruler in that age could lay claim, on which he received every symbolic and religious assurance which the century knew."[51]

If we take our stand at the coronation of Henry III in 1028, eleven years before his father's death, we can only wonder at the strength of the German monarchy. Compared with the France of Robert II it was a homogenous land, held together by solid traditions, ruled by energetic and intelligent sovereigns.[52] The leadership of Europe was firmly established in German hands.[53] Nor was this power and predominance based on weak foundations. The Ottonian and Salian emperors were not merely holding down the cowed but ultimately invincible forces of particularism and princely egotism. The weaknesses which are so often alleged to have been

---

[51] Schramm, 213—214.

[52] On the personal superiority of the German rulers of the period to those of France, cf. Reynaud, 111—112.—For Germany under Henry III, cf. P. Kehr, " Vier Kapitel aus d. Gesch. Kaiser Heinrichs III," *Abhandl. d. preuss. Akademie*, 1930, *Phil.-hist. Kl.*, No. III.

[53] Cf. A. Cartellieri, *Die Weltstellung d. deutschen Reiches*, 911—1047 (1932), and in summary, *Machtpolitik vor den Kreuzzügen* (1935).

eating away the roots of the monarchical tree were
non-existent. The " stem-duchy," we have seen,
never developed into a constitutional actuality. The
crown was not beset by a destructive conception of
electoral monarchy. It is true that Germany in
919, like every other country in Europe, still needed
welding more firmly together; but this was not on
account of a unique tribal organization, strongly
resistant to centralization, but because, like every
other country in Europe, the dominions subject to
the German king had suffered the ravages of invasion
from north and east. Nowhere else, however, had
the monarchy shown itself more competent to resist
and counteract the resultant disintegration. Something has been said of its political measures[54]; but
more important and more effective was what we
may broadly call its " cultural " policy.[55] A constant interchange of personalities broke down
local bounds and local feeling. Already under
Otto I a monk of Reichenau became abbot of
St. Maurice in Magdeburg and subsequently
bishop of Hildesheim, while the Saxon Hildeward
received at St. Gallen the education which he
was later to convert to good account in Saxony
as bishop of Halberstadt.[56] Regensburg became
a connecting link between north and south:
Bamberg, the bishopric created by Henry II, was
as important culturally as politically.[57] The zeal
and fervour embodied in the German reform movements of the eleventh century—movements which,
influenced though they may have been by Cluniac

[54] *Supra*, 35—38, 42.
[55] This aspect of the situation has been very brilliantly summarized
by M. Seidlmayer, *Deutscher Nord u. Süd im Hochmittelalter* (1928).
[56] Seidlmayer, 45—46.
[57] *Ibid.*, 80, 82.

inspiration, quickly developed along independent lines and produced specifically German fruits from roots growing deep in German soil[58]—were used by Henry II and Henry III to bind the land together, and under Henry IV the Hirsau congregation performed the same task.[59]   By the time of Henry II cultural interchanges between north and south were so frequent and normal that the citation of examples would give a false impression: it was no longer a question of isolated personalities but of a broad and solid movement.[60]   As the eleventh century proceeded regional differences gradually fell into the background:[61] it was then that the collective name for the German people, *Teutonici*, rapidly became usual.[62] Even the Saxons who rose in rebellion " pro libertate, pro legibus, pro patria sua " in 1073, showed no inclination to resist the rule of Conrad II and Henry III or to stand apart, under the first two Salian kings, from the rest of Germany.[63]   By the middle of the eleventh century the realm was firmly united under its ruling dynasty and all traces of particularism seemed dead.

The unity and solidarity under the crown which is apparent at the middle of the eleventh century

---

[58] Seidlmayer, 74, 98—99.—It is necessary to emphasize this fact in view of the constant tendency to regard all these movements, and Hirsau in particular, as merely off-shoots of Cluny (e.g. Reynaud, 197). This view—which plays a large part in Reynaud's fantastic conception of a mediaeval Germany dominated by French influences—was adequately and fairly dealt with by Hauck, *Kirchengesch.* III, 460, 514, 864—876.

[59] Seidlmayer, 89—90. Cf. Kehr, 14, on the effects of royal ecclesiastical foundations and endowments in spreading the renown and tradition of the royal dynasty throughout the land.

[60] Seidlmayer. 93.

[61] *Ibid.*, 72.

[62] *Ibid.*, 65.

[63] Seidlmayer, 61.   " Der sächsische Stamm ertrug die Herrschaft des zweiten Saliers ebenso willig wie die des ersten," says Steindorff (*Jahrbücher Heinrichs des Dritten* II, 366.)

was due, as is well known, in a special degree to the co-operation of leading churchmen and the harmonious relations between church and crown.[64] But if the fact is well known, it remains true that there is scarcely any chapter of German history which is so little understood as the relations of crown and church before the Investiture Contest.[65] In England and elsewhere where ULRICH STUTZ's thorough studies of pre-Gregorian ecclesiastical institutions have never been sufficiently appreciated, these relationships are still seen through partisan Hildebrandine eyes, the Gregorian thesis that the royal position in the church was built on usurpation and violence is still too unhesitatingly adopted. We have to realize, in the first place, that before the creation of a Roman canon law there was a consistent body of Germanic canon law, accepted by all parties, which took a very different attitude from later legislation both to the laity and to the rights of the laity in the church;[66] and the essential element of this Germanic law was the proprietary right of the lord over the churches he had founded and over their lands. It is this paramount overlordship, and not the strong hand of irreligious monarchs, which explains the interference of German rulers in the internal administration of the German church during the tenth and eleventh centuries. They are exercising a right, not abusing a power. But they are also performing a duty. For we have to realize, in the second place, that the king was no mere layman. By his consecration—which had all the significance of a sacrament

[64] Cf. Joachimsen, *infra* II, 99 sqq.

[65] This subject will be dealt with in its broad European aspect, in G. Tellenbach's volume, *Church, State and Christian Society at the time of the Investiture Contest*, to be published in this series.

[66] Cf. *infra* II, 35—70.

until, at the earliest, the middle of the twelfth century[67]—he was constituted *rex et sacerdos*,[68] and his
sacerdotal position not only made him, as we have
seen,[69] the chosen mediator between clergy and
people, but also imposed on him the duty of " ruling "
his church.[70]   Thus Henry III could reply to a radical
bishop: " Ego vero similiter sacro oleo data mihi
prae caeteris imperandi potestate sum pe. runctus."[71]
To regard the relations of church and state in tenth
and eleventh century Germany as an " alliance "
against the lay princes is therefore a falsification.
The king did not need to ally with a church which
was tied to him by proprietary and sacerdotal bonds:
it was his church and he was its divinely appointed
ruler.

The German monarch could therefore use the
church, not as an unwilling tool diverted from its
proper function, but as an instrument placed by
God in royal hands for the work of civilization and
social organization, regarding the objects of which
church and state were still as one.   It is often stated
that ecclesiastical co-operation was only obtained
at a great price, at a cost which ultimately ruined
the monarchy.   The immediate political advantage
of Henry II's creation of Bamberg and Henry III's
support of Bremen, for example, is obvious enough
and does not fail to win recognition;[72] but the king,
it is said, was only raising up powers which were

---

[67] Schramm, *Krönung*, 256.

[68] On the conception *rex et sacerdos*, cf. in summary, Kern, 85—86,
and Schramm, *English Coronation*, 115—121; for Henry III, cf. Kehr,
12, and *infra* II, 104.

[69] *Supra*, 53.

[70] The word *regere* appears twice in this sense in the coronation-order
of Mainz (§§ 7, 28); cf. Schramm, *Krönung*, 272.

[71] *Gesta epp. Leodensium* II. 66 (MG. *Script.* VII, 230).

[72] Cf. Thompson, *Feudal Germany*, 50—51 (Bamberg), and 184—187
(Bremen); cf. *infra* II, 86.

bound, in the end, to turn against himself or his successors. Against this view, however, it must be insisted—even at the risk of stating the obvious—that no king in the first half of the eleventh century could foresee the attack which was to be made in the next generation on what, for three hundred years and more, had been unquestioningly accepted as the rightful and firmly established relationship of church and state.[73] It could not be foreseen that the state's paramount ownership of the lands of the " national church "[74] would be called in question, and that the direct administrative control, which was the corollary of such ownership, would be transformed, after the Concordat of Worms, into an indirect feudal overlordship.[75] But the tendency to apply Hildebrandine ideas to an age in which they had no following is not the only reason why the Ottonian and Salian kings are supposed to have sacrificed their ultimate prospects to their more immediate advantage. More significant still, is a radically mistaken conception of the connected institutions of " immunity " and " advocacy ".[76] If the immunity, which played so large a part in German governmental organization in the middle ages, was simply exemption from state control, and if the advocate was an official of the immune church, who took the place of the count[77] and was responsible

[73] This essential point has once again been emphasized by Rörig, 8—9.
[74] Cf. particularly J. Ficker, " Über das Eigenthum des Reichs am Reichskirchengute," *Sitz.-Ber. d. Wiener Akademie, Phil.-hist. Kl.* LXXII (1872), 55—146.
[75] Cf. Mitteis, *infra* II, 242.
[76] Cf. M. Kroell, *L'immunité franque* (1910); E. E. Stengel, *Die Immunität in Deutschland bis z. Ende d.* 11. *Jahrhunderts*; H. Hirsch, *Die Klosterimmunität seit dem Investiturstreit* (1913); A. Waas, *Vogtei u. Bede in d. deutschen Kaiserzeit* I (1919); E. F. Otto, *Die Entwicklung d. deutschen Kirchenvogtei im* 10. *Jahrhundert* (1933), few of whose arguments, however, can be accepted.
[77] The question whether exemption from the count's jurisdiction

E

to the church as the count was responsible to the king, it is obvious that the creation of immunities on a large scale—and this fact stands altogether beyond dispute[78]—must rapidly lead to a dislocation and disintegration of government. But neither supposition is true. It is essential in the first place to understand that—in this regard as in others[79]— the mediaeval German constitution and its specific institutions were anything but a direct, unaltered continuation of the Frankish or Carolingian constitution.[80] Whatever the Frankish advocate may have been,[81] the theory that the advocate was an "official" of the church which he represented, only entered German history with the growth of the reform movement in the eleventh century,[82] and was not really successful—so far as it was successful at all[83]— until the thirteenth century.[84] In the earlier period the advocate is a lord, exercising lordly powers over the church's dependents closely connected, if not

(Otto, 3) was complete or not, cannot be discussed here. In fact, it appears that jurisdiction in questions of life and limb belonged to the count, but was of small importance, since it was still rarely exercised (Hirsch, HG., 123—125): the development of a public criminal jurisdiction—as opposed to the private "wergeld" system of compensation—belongs in all essentials to a later age (HG., II. iv). It was of immense constitutional importance, since—in spite of the efforts of the monarchy (ibid., 234—235) —the new jurisdiction passed into the hands of the advocates, and so transformed and heightened their powers. But this was a new phase in the history of the advocacy, which hardly began before the twelfth century.

[78] Waas, 120.

[79] Cf. supra, 4, 24. We shall have to return to the point in connexion with the county organization; infra, 81.

[80] It is one of Otto's merits to have emphasized this fact (pp. 154-5).

[81] Cf. for example, H. v. Schubert, Gesch. d. christlichen Kirche im Frühmittelalter (1921), 554—555, 560.

[82] Waas rightly points out (pp. 6—7) that the extraordinary emphasis on the official capacity of the advocate in monastic charters of the late eleventh and twelfth centuries—and above all in forged charters—is itself a suspicious circumstance, and an indication that it is a novelty which the monasteries are trying to introduce.

[83] On the whole question, cf. Hirsch, infra II, 145—173.

[84] Cf. Spindler, Anfänge d. bayer. Landesfürstentums, 117.

identical,[85] with the proprietary rights which the proprietary lord possessed in the church's lands. The immunity, also, is not the *emunitas* which had found its way from Roman into Merovingian institutions.[86] The charters themselves use other less antiquarian terms, *defensio*, *tuitio*, *mundeburdium*, to describe the institution,[87] and *mundeburdium*—the special protection and authority exercised by a lord over his household and his household dependents—is the essence of the institution, as it develops after the accession of Louis the Pious in 813.[88] A grant of "immunity" to a church or monastery, therefore, means its inclusion in the household of the king, implies that it shares the special protection and the special relationship with the crown with which the royal household was favoured.[89] Far from loosening the ties between the monarchy and the churches, immunity created a new bond, stronger than the ordinary administrative connexion: it "exempted" churches from the ordinary county administration, but only in order to place them under the more direct authority, the *mundeburdium*, of the king. And this was the sense and purpose of the whole institution. Threatened in the first half of the tenth century by the possibility of the growth of a regional or "tribal"

---

[85] Cf. Planitz, ZRG. *Germ. Abt.* XLI (1920), 428—432, and Aubin, *Vierteljahrschr. f. Sozial- u. Wirtschaftsgesch.* XVI (1922), 409—414.

[86] It would, as Waas points out (pp. 100—101), be remarkable, if "eine Steuerbefreiung des römischen Rechts" had possessed the force "lange Jahrhunderte nach der Zerstörung des römischen Reichs die Grundlage der deutschen Verfassung des Mittelalters zu werden . . . neue Beamten, neue Gerichtsbezirke und schliesslich neue staatliche Gebilde zu schaffen." Waas, 102.

[87] Waas, 102.

[88] For the whole question, cf. Waas, cap. II, § 6; and cf. Stutz, *infra* II, 59.

[89] On the household, cf. Rosenstock, cap. III. It was as members of the royal household, and not as princes of the realm, that bishops took part in public life in Ottonian times; cf. Rosenstock, 26, 54 (n. 32), and Otto, 158–9.

church organization,[90] the monarchy bound the churches of the realm to itself by the " immunity " and thus acquired a new means of unifying the realm. Possessed of the *mundeburdium*, the king had the right to appoint or to participate in the appointment of bishops and abbots, and the result was the appointment of bishops who had graduated through the royal chapel[91] and were imbued with the same conscientious spirit as Henry II himself.[92] Possessed of the *mundeburdium*, the king was himself the supreme advocate of the imperial churches, and the local advocates who performed the actual duties of the office were only his subordinates and representatives.[93] Even where the right to " elect " the local advocate was granted to a monastery or bishopric, the king, as supreme advocate, retained the right to " constitute " him in office—his authority, in other words, derived from the crown, and the king maintained control, for *electio* was a preliminary, *constitutio* the decisive stage in appointment.[94]

[90] *Supra*, 37, 39.

[91] Cf. W. Gesler, *Der Berichte des Monachus Hamerslebiensis über die kaiserliche Kapelle* (1915); S. Görlitz, *Die deutsche Hofkapelle im Zeitalter der Sachsen u. Salier* (1936); H. W. Klewitz, " Cancellaria," *Deutsches Archiv f. Gesch. d. Mittelalters* I (1937), 64; Kehr, *Vier Kapitel*, 10, 29.

[92] Deusdedit (*Contra invasores* II. 15) calls the royal chapel the " seminarium symoniacae hereseos et totius christianae religionis lamentabilem destructionem; " but even the brief glimpse of the work of the Ottonian and Salian episcopacy afforded by Seidlmayer (pp. 73—89) or by Macdonald (*Authority and Reason in the Early Middle Ages*, 1933, 76—95) indicates that Sigebert of Gembloux was less blinded by partisan passion than Deusdedit, when he wrote (*Vita Deod. Metten.*, c. 7): " Iure felicia dixerim Ottonis tempora, cum claris praesulibus et sapientibus viris respublica sit reformata, pax ecclesiarum reformata, honestas religionis redintegrata. Erat videre et re ipsa probare, verum esse illud philosophi: fortunatum esse rempublicam, si vel reges saperent vel regnarent sapientes. Praeerant enim populo regni non mercennarii sed pastores clarissimi."

[93] Waas, 68—77, 120.

[94] Cf. Waas, 124: " advocatus, quem ipse ad hoc opus a regia potestate constituendum elegerit," " advocato ad hoc opus de abbate electo et a regia potestate constituto." Otto, 158, refers to Otto I's charter for Magdeburg, with provision for " free election " *nostro consensu.*—Schmid,

These ideas applied from the beginning to the churches of which the monarchy was founder and over which it therefore exercised proprietary rights. But as the proprietary régime gradually gained ground and was applied, as the prevailing system, to churches which had come into the king's hands in other ways,[95] the ideas that went with it were extended also, and by the time of Henry II the ancient bishoprics were treated as standing under the royal *mundeburdium* and subject to the king's advocacy.[96] Thus the organization of all churches directly dependent on the crown was consolidated, and at the same time the attempt was made to extend the bounds of the " royal " or "imperial " or " national " church, until all the churches of the realm were united in one body. This was the ultimate meaning of the numerous concessions of immunity to churches founded by the lay nobility: a grant of immunity and protection and freedom meant that immunity, that protection and that freedom which was assured by membership of the *Reichskirche*, the " national church "—it signified the end of the proprietary rights of the lay lord and incorporation in the great ecclesiastical body which the king alone ruled.[97] Nor was the laity in ignorance of this intention: "regalem nolui facere, nisi coactus," wrote Ulrich of Lenzburg in 1036, but he could not withstand the dual pressure of the crown, striving to unite the German church, and of the canons, seeking the *libertas* which the crown alone could give, and by 1045 his family foundation of Beromünster

Kanon. Wahl, 36, etc., has explained how and why the conception of *libera electio* comprised royal participation.

[95] Cf. Stutz, *infra* II, 61.

[96] Waas, 159; Aubin, 412; G. Weise, *Königtum u. Bischofswahl im fränk. u. deutschen Reich vor dem Investiturstreit* (1912), 103, 111—112, 127.

[97] Hirsch, *infra* II, 136, 150, 170.

had become a royal priory.[68] Thus the monarchy
in the eleventh century was gradually welding
together a united German church and—more than
this—a united imperial church, immunity and advocacy were being extended until they comprehended
the whole eclesiastical organization of the empire
from the Holy See[99] to the smallest monastery.[100]
Closely attached to the royal household and through
the household to the king himself, under the control
of the supreme royal advocate—a control reaffirmed,
for all who were spiritually minded, by the king's
sacerdotal character—the church was more firmly
attached to the monarchy than ever before. Immunity and advocacy, in short, had proved their
value as centralizing forces, as institutions which were
building up the resources of the central government
and increasing the crown's hold over the land.

But it would not be correct to regard the strength
of the Ottonian and Salian monarchy as based exclusively on the church and on the fidelity and
good-will of the bishops. It is easy, but it is false
to say that the crown relied solely on the prelates
and that when they deserted it—whether the king
could have foreseen the desertion, hardly matters
from this point of view—it had no other resources
on which to draw. On the contrary, the development
of the organs of central government begins very
markedly under Otto I.[101] There was, of course, no
separately organized chancery at this period;[102] but

[98] Hirsch, *Klosterimmunität*, 7—8; Waas, 171.
[99] *Infra* II, 64; but it is mistaken to suppose that the Holy See was
ever treated as one of the emperor's proprietary churches, even in the days
of Henry III; cf. Stutz, ZRG. *Kanon. Abt.* XX (1931), 649—650.
[100] Waas, 173.
[101] This side of Otto's work is too rarely emphasized; cf. Haller, HZ.
CLIV, 343.
[102] Klewitz (*op. cit.*) has shown that the growth of the chancery, as
a separate office of state, out of the *capella* only occurs—in Germany as

the reorganization which succeeded the rebellion of 953—955 brought a new consistency and vigour into the routine of government. The supreme office of *archicapellanus*, the control of the whole clerical staff of the royal household, which in the previous half-century had been disputed between Mainz, Cologne, Trier and Salzburg, passed to Otto's brother, Bruno, the archbishop of Cologne, and to his son, William, the archbishop of Mainz, and on Bruno's death in 965, was permanently attached to the see of Mainz.[103] At the same time a new permanent official, the *cancellarius*, was placed in charge of the clerical work, responsible to the *archicapellanus* and controlling the clerks engaged in the written work of government.[104] But most important of all is the sudden increase in the number of notaries or clerks. From the beginning of Henry I's reign until 956 only one or two clerks seem to have been deputed at one time to carry out the writing of charters: in 956 the number suddenly rises to as many as eight, and all were men who performed a long period of service.[105] This change reflects the growth of settled government and the increasing activity of the monarchy. Permanence of machinery—expressed particularly in the establishment of the office of chancellor—meant permanence and continuity of governmental tradition.

elsewhere—at the end of the twelfth or the beginning of the thirteenth century. Nevertheless he seems (p. 58) to underrate the significance of the changes which took place under Otto I.

[103] Erben, *Die Kaiser- u. Königsurkunden des Mittelalters* (Below—Meinecke, *Handbuch d. mittelalterl. u. neueren Gesch.*, 1907), 56—57.—For the following, cf. H. Bresslau, *Handbuch d. Urkundenlehre* I (2nd ed.), 424—428.

[104] Erben, 71.—The term *cancellarius* had, of course, been in general use from Carolingian times onwards (Bresslau, 377 sqq.), but simply as a synonym for *notarius*, and this untechnical use of the word continued as late as the time of Henry I (Bresslau, 423). Cf. Erben, 65, 67, 69, etc.

[105] Erben, 98.

The development of local administration came
later, but was no less significant of the constructive
powers of the monarchy. Its main feature was the
development of the *ministerialis* class as the nucleus
of a royal bureaucracy.[106] The great administrative
programme of the Salian period, which was first
vividly described by KARL WILHELM NITZSCH, is,
however, too well known to need detailed examination:[107] two essential points were centralization of
government in Goslar and the revindication and
closer organization and exploitation of the crown
lands, but the key to the whole was the building up
of a ministerial bureaucracy, which could be trusted
to put the programme into effect. This use of the
ministerial class, however, is only one side of the
general tendency of the Salian rulers to draw away
from the nobility—the small group of freeborn men
in whose hands long tradition had placed the sum of
governmental power—and make contact with the
unfree but socially and economically rising classes,
the peasants and the townspeople.[108] It was no
accident of history that the Rhenish towns were
among the staunchest supporters of Henry IV
throughout the rebellions of his reign,[109] or that the
Landfrieden of 1103 gave special attention to the
legal position of the servile peasant class.[110] It is

[106] Cf. Joachimsen, *infra* II, 110 sqq.—On the *ministeriales* in general
cf. *infra* II, 209 sqq., 262 sqq., and the brief statement in Thompson,
Feudal Germany, 324 sqq., or in Blondel, *Etude sur la politique de l'empereur
Frédéric II en Allemagne* (1892), 118—126. The recent arguments of
E. F. Otto, *Adel u. Freiheit im deutschen Staat des Mittelalters. Studien
über nobiles u. Ministerialen* (1937), cannot be regarded as probative; cf.
Stutz, *Sitz.-Ber. d. preuss. Akademie, Phil.-hist. Kl.* (1937), 240—248.

[107] In addition to Joachimsen, cf. Thompson, 185 sqq., 330 sqq.,
346 sqq., 350 sqq.

[108] Hirsch, HG., 139, 230, 232—235; cf. *infra* II, 113, 152.

[109] Cf. for example, Rörig, *Bürgertum u. Staat in d. älteren deutschen
Gesch.* (1928), 7—8.

[110] Hirsch, HG., 138, 234.

true that, in all this process, only a beginning was made during the period between Henry II and Henry IV; but that beginning is enough to show the vitality of the monarchy and its ability to adapt itself to new social conditions. It is essential to insist on this fact, which we have also observed in the development of immunity and advocacy and of the *Eigenkirchenwesen*, because it is still too often stated that the government of the Saxons and Salians was simply a restoration of the Carolingian régime, a pure reaction, antiquarian in spirit, sterile, lacking in original power, incapable of development.[111] That this view overrates the durability of Carolingian institutions, and particularly of the county system, goes without saying;[112] but it also underrates the vigour and spontaneity of German public life in the tenth and eleventh centuries, and particularly the vitality incorporated in the monarchy. Far from representing a period in which an obsolescent system was sinking into decay, the age of Henry II, Conrad II and Henry III sees the monarchy already grasping at the opportunities which the rise of new classes to political importance was creating. It was already on the path which fifty years and more later the Norman rulers were to tread in England, and which the Capetians were hardly to reach before the second half of the twelfth century.

[111] Cf. particularly Reynaud, 131—141, 254, 368, etc.
[112] Cf. for example, Th. Mayer, *infra* II, 7—9.

IV

THE COUNTY AND THE PRINCIPALITY

The main object of the last two chapters has been to show that the German monarchy of the earlier middle ages was not, as is usually supposed, hampered from its very inception by two specific forces—the "stem-duchy" and the elective theory of kingship—which no other rulers had to face, and saddled with an obsolete system of government which was bound sooner or later to collapse. We have now followed some of the main developments of German constitutional life from the beginning of the tenth century to the crisis which followed the death of Henry III in 1056. We have seen that the heritage of Henry III was as capable of healthy development, as full of potentialities, as the England of William the Conqueror or Henry I and the France of Philip I or Louis VI. And yet it is only too well known that the potentialities which were evident enough in 1056 never developed into realities. How was it, it has been asked,[1] that the German empire, which stood at the height of its power in 1046 when Henry III set Suitger of Bamberg on the papal throne as Clement II, was forced only half a century later, in the days of Urban II, to leave the leadership of Christendom in the First Crusade in French hands? Why was "German power transformed in such a remarkably short time into German powerlessness"?[2] If the causes had been merely political,

[1] Cartellieri, *Machtpolitik vor den Kreuzzügen* (1935).
[2] *Ibid.*, 6. Cartellieri looks to the changes in the international situation for an answer; but, important as the European balance of power is,

ultimate recovery would have been possible: and yet, in spite of the administrative abilities and governmental reforms of the Hohenstaufen, the monarchy never again attained the calm security which it seemed to possess under Henry III. The Investiture Contest without doubt marks a turning point in German history, though the conflict with the church is as much the occasion as the cause of the crisis. And the most characteristic feature of the transition is not the decline of royal power—it would be hard, in view of the achievements of Frederick Barbarossa's reign, to speak of more than a temporary decline in the power of the monarchy—but the rise of new powers which, after two centuries of crisis when the whole future of Germany hung in the balance, were eventually to achieve predominance. What begins, dimly but discernibly, in the reign of Henry IV is, in short, the rise of the territorial principalities.

The historical development of Germany between 911 and 1077 is apt to be befogged by false conceptions which—by summarizing the work of recent scholars—we have tried to dispel; but the essential facts, misinterpreted though they often are, are well known. For the period between 1077 and 1250, on the other hand, even the facts sink into the background, and German internal development is treated as a mere by-product of the greater imperial question, the whole period is seen as one long contest between a grandiose imperial policy, pursued at German expense by the Hohenstaufen, and an attempt to devise a strictly German policy, in which the Welfs, Lothar and Henry the Lion, are supposed to have

it only reflects the more fundamental changes in the internal balance of power within the countries concerned.

been the leaders.[3] For a hundred and fifty years, it is implied, Germany stood still, awaiting the result of a contest which was fought on Italian soil. It is not our place here to consider the course and import of imperial policy in the twelfth century,[4] or to attempt once again the futile task of weighing its influence on German development. One incident alone may be noted in passing: the events of 1176—1180 which led to the fall of Henry the Lion, and which have so long been regarded as the classic example of the influence of Italian affairs over German destiny. Was Henry the Lion's refusal of aid in 1176, as has so long been thought, the result of opposition to a non-German policy? Was Barbarossa in 1180 revenging the defeat of Legnano, for which Henry the Lion was chiefly responsible? We cannot review all the theories which historians from GIESE-BRECHT onwards have put forward to explain the fall of the Saxon duke;[5] but it is important—for the case is representative of much else in this complicated period—to note that the view now established and generally accepted traces the breach to a purely

[3] Cf. among many others, Thompson, cap. VIII, where this antithesis is pushed to fantastic extremes. No useful purpose would be served by detailed criticism of Thompson's hypotheses. His conception of Lothar of Supplinburg (pp. 272—274) is so far from reality that it cannot be measured by historical standards; his conception of Barbarossa, " infatuated with the grandiose idea of mediaeval imperialism " and pursuing " a ' rule or ruin ' policy " (p. 275), suffering from " caesaristic madness " and a " mania for application of the Roman law " (p. 277), obsessed by " egotism, megalomania, *Weltmacht* " (p. 289), only needs comparing with the sure methodic investigations of Hohenstaufen internal policy in the second volume of this work to be revealed in its true light as specious and superficial.

[4] Cf. W. Lenel's classic essay on the Italian policy of Frederick Barbarossa, HZ. CXXVIII, 189—261.

[5] They are conveniently summarized by F. Güterbock, " Barbarossa u. Heinrich d. Löwe," *Vergangenheit u. Gegenwart* XXIII (1933), 261—264, in the course of a very balanced and moderate survey of the relations of the two men throughout their lives.—Besides the two explanations mentioned in the text, it has been suggested that the breach between emperor and duke was caused (i) by Henry's foreign relations, particularly with England, (ii) by the question of the succession to Welf VI's lands.

German matter: the question of Goslar.[6] One of
the richest towns of Germany,[7] closely identified with
the monarchy from the days of Henry III,[8] and
particularly important in the twelfth century as one
of the few remaining strongholds which the Swabian
rulers retained in the north,[9] the question was simply
whether the crown was going to retain this essential
pillar of its northern power, or whether Goslar was
to be swallowed up in the vast territorial agglomeration which Henry the Lion was building up and
welding together. It was a test case for Frederick;
for the loss of Goslar meant the destruction of one
of the few vantage-points from which the " terri-
torialisation " of the north could be held in check.
And it was characteristic that Henry the Lion
should be brought to nothing by an incident of this
sort; for his whole energy was concentrated on building up a territorial principality by petty aggression.
But his territorial policy, so successful against smaller
men, was the cause of his downfall when it brought
him up against a prince more powerful than himself.[10]
And yet the political importance of the events of
1180 must not be exaggerated. Henry the Lion,
though by far the greatest, was only one of the new
princes, who, rising on the tide of the social and
intellectual revolution which the Investiture Contest

[6] Cf. in particular H. Niese, HZ. CXII (1914), 551—553.

[7] Hildebrand, 309, 329.

[8] *Supra*, 72; Kehr, 8.

[9] Seidlmayer, 102.

[10] Hildebrand's conclusion (p. 300) is the very opposite: " Heinrich
der Löwe ist nicht an seiner Territorialpolitik gescheitert." But here,
as at many other points throughout the book, the idealization not merely
of Henry himself but also of all his actions, and a certain unwillingness
to see anything in his territorial policy but a perfectly conceived scheme,
which only failed because (p. 301) " the times were not ripe for his grandiose
plans," has blinded the author to the limitations of Henry's policy and
its opportunist character; cf. Hüttebräuker, ZRG. *Germ. Abt.* LVII,
574 sqq.

had stimulated,[11] were striving after regalian rights
and sovereign powers. His fall in 1180 might have
been a turning point, if the monarchy had been able
to use it as the starting point for a rigidly executed
policy of territorial recuperation;[12] but this, in spite
of beginnings under Henry VI and again under
Frederick II[1],[3] it was unable to do. Thus the
position which Henry the Lion vacated in 1180 was
handed on without apparent diminution to those
among whom his fiefs were divided, and the problem,
instead of being solved, was left to work itself out.
Already in 1180, in short, the territorial powers
which had risen in the revolutionary period a century
before, were too strong for the monarchy. It could
triumph over Henry the Lion, but not over the principles which Henry the Lion blindly represented.

The Hohenstaufen rulers nevertheless made re-
solute endeavours to cope with the problem. Their
constitutional policy, finely conceived, courageously
applied and full of high prospects, is their chief claim
to respect and admiration: it is this policy which
makes Frederick Barbarossa and Henry II of England
not merely contemporaries but equal partners in
the one great task of setting government on a new
foundation. What was this policy? Why did it
fail? What were the forces opposed to it and whence
did they draw their strength? All these questions
are dealt with fully and satisfactorily in the essays
which follow; and we can therefore leave the answer
to them. But of the three preliminary questions
which we set ourselves to solve at the beginning of
this introduction, of the three hypotheses which had
to be cleared out of the way in order that the attitude

[11] Cf. Brackmann, *infra* II, 286 sqq.
[12] Cf. Mitteis, *Politische Prozesse*, 115, 123.
[13] Cf. *infra*, 129.

of the writers whose work is assembled in the following volume might be rendered more easily comprehensible, one still remains and must be considered in this connexion: the view that the new territorial principalities, consolidated by the usurpation of royal rights, were based on the old counties, that the new prince was the old count writ large.[14] It is this development of the count's powers which is usually regarded as the link between the period before and the period after the Investiture Contest. Already under Henry II and Conrad II, it is pointed out,[15] the heritability of countships was a recognized fact. The Investiture Contest made it impossible for the crown to revoke this development—indeed, it so weakened the monarchy that the counts were able to amass new rights. Thus firmly ensconced in an unassailable position at the beginning of the twelfth century, they had only to weaken the crown by active and passive opposition, in order to become territorial princes. The question was one of relative power, and in the end the monarchy proved the weaker of the two forces.

The correctness or the falsity of this point of view can only be proved by minute investigations into the territorial formation of each separate principality; and it goes without saying that the results of such investigations will differ widely in different localities. But one essential fact can now be regarded as established:[16] the decline of the old county organiza-

[14] *Supra*, 23.

[15] Cf. Thompson, 311, citing Giesebrecht II, 70, 284, 594, 625.

[16] It is impossible to cite more than one or two of the more outstanding works on the rise of the principalities: cf. for example, H. Aubin, *Die Entstehung der Landeshoheit nach niederrheinischen Quellen* (1920), E. Freiherr v. Guttenberg, *Die Territorialbildung am Obermain* (1926), A. Gasser, *Die Entstehung u. Ausbildung d. Landeshoheit im Gebiet der Schweizer Eidgenossenschaft* (1930), H. Eberhardt, *Die Anfänge des Territorialfürstentums in Nordthüringen* (1932), H. W. Klewitz, *Studien z. territorialen*

tion. This can be observed from two different standpoints: on the one hand, there is increasing looseness in the application of the term *comecia*, which comes to mean nothing more than jurisdiction of the most indeterminate sort,[17] and on the other hand, the counties of the twelfth century are only rarely coterminous with the counties of Carolingian or Saxon Germany.[18] It is, of course, undeniable that a particular district might remain stable and undivided for generations, particularly if it remained in the hands of one family; but the trend of historical development led, in fact, in the opposite direction, and such factors as the growth of immunities or the division of inheritances produced a rapid sub-division of the old judicial and administrative organization. The evolution of the class from which the counts were drawn,[19] on the other hand, brought with it a reorganization. When the great noble families of early mediaeval Germany finally divided into a multitude of branches in the twelfth century, each branch began the work of reorganizing its holdings into one

Entwicklung des Bistums Hildesheim (1932), M. Spindler, *Die Anfänge d. bayerischen Landesfürstentums* (1937).—R. Hildebrand, *Der sächsische "Staat" Heinrichs d. Löwen* (1937), 49—50, 62, etc., clings to the old view that the Frankish county organization remained intact and provided the territorial basis for the principalities, although v. Below himself had categorically rejected this hypothesis; cf. G. v. Below, *Vom Mittelalter z. Neuzeit* (1924), 24—25.—For a general statement, cf. Mitteis, *infra* II, 267 sqq.; G. v. Below, " Der Ursprung d. Landeshoheit," *Territorium u. Stadt* (2nd ed., 1923), 1—52; Th. Knapp, " Zur Gesch. d. Landeshoheit," *Württembergische Vierteljahrshefte f. Landesgesch.* XXXVIII (1932), 9—112.

[17] Klewitz, 22: thus a village or even a mere manor is conveyed *cum comecia*. Cf. also Knapp, 40.

[18] Aubin, 39—40, Eberhardt, 20—22, Klewitz, 26. Spindler, 145, is more conservative; but the examples which he cites on p. 139 to show connexion between the later administrative units and the old counties, all prove the dismemberment of the old divisions. Moreover, it must be remembered that the Carolingian counties were never organized as a series of compact geographical blocks with distinct boundaries and a specific territorial competence: the count's authority was over persons, not over land, and many counties probably never took shape as distinct geographical divisions. Cf. Klewitz, 9, 15, Spindler, 13.

[19] Cf. v. Dungern, *infra* II, 208 sq., 217, 222.

F

compact honour, administered as a unit, no matter what was the origin of the various components from which it was formed.[20] At the same time they took— no doubt as an expression of their new power—the title of count;[21] but the new count was not the old count and the new county was not the old county. A patent, if external, sign of this change is the fact that the new counts, from highest to lowest, call themselves after their family castles[22]—a reflection of the establishment of the *Burgbezirk* or "castellany" as the normal unit of administration;[23] and still another sign is the disappearance of the old *Dingstätte*, of the traditional centres for the assembly of the county court,[24] and the centralization of local government round new administrative points.[25] The reorganization of government under Frederick Barbarossa was, indeed, based in a large degree on the recognition of these new administrative districts and their subordination within the feudal hierarchy:[26] in this way they were to be brought into dependence on the crown. But this reorganization was only

[20] Spindler, 146–7. Cf. Hirsch, MIÖG. XXXV (1914), 76: " Seit dem Beginn des 12. Jahrhunderts verschwindet allmählich die Nennung der Gaue, dafür nennen sich die Dynasten nach ihrer Stammburg, die nun zum Mittelpunkt ihrer Herrschaftsgerechtsame wird. Im übrigen waren dies kein einheitlicher Begriff, sondern ein Konglomerat aus gräflichen Rechten und hohen Vogteien, grundherrlichen und Eigenkirchenrechten. Das war eben die erste Aufgabe der territorialen Bildung, an Stelle dieser verschiedenen Rechtstitel eine einheitliche Rechtsanschauung zu setzen." Cf. Knapp, 36.

[21] Cf. particularly J. Friedrichs, *Burg u. territoriale Grafschaften* (1907).

[22] Thus the emperor Lothar (1125—1127) was the first of his family officially named after the Supplingenburg; cf. Hildebrand, 192. For other examples cf. Hildebrand, 73 (Waldeck), Spindler, 13 (Bogen), Aubin, 42 (Saffenburg).

[23] Cf. *infra*, 85 sqq.

[24] Klewitz, 17, 26, Spindler, 140—141, 143, 146.

[25] Niese, *Die Verwaltung des Reichsgutes im 13. Jahrhundert* (1905), 58 sqq., 168 sqq., 243 sqq., has described the organisation of the new *officia* instituted by the Hohenstaufen in their own demesnes. Cf. also Weller, *Württ. Vierteljahrshefte f. Landesgesch.* XXXVI (1930), 163 sqq.; Hildebrand, 385 sqq.; Spindler, 132 sqq.

[26] Cf. *infra* II, 229.

necessary because the old county organization had gradually given way to a more modern network of administrative districts.

Historically, therefore, there are good reasons to think that the permanence of the Frankish county organization has been exaggerated, and that it cannot have played the part in the formation of the later principalities which has so often been attributed to it. That does not mean, on the other hand, that the rights which had been exercised by the counts, however they may have been divided and reconstituted, may not have been the ultimate source of the sovereign powers subsequently exercised by the territorial princes. This, it is well known, is the view vigorously and consistently maintained by GEORG VON BELOW,[27] and directed in particular against those historians who have maintained that territorial power, richness in demesnes, was more important than rights, that the sovereignty of the later princes sprang from *Grundherrschaft* or landed proprietorship. But it may immediately be said that VON BELOW's view, although it contains many elements of truth, is no longer accepted without radical qualifications. It is clear, in the first place, that rights without power behind them will always remain empty rights; and in the struggles of the twelfth, thirteenth and fourteenth centuries, when an untold number of petty potentates, who all started on a legal equality, were aspiring to princely powers, what raised one dynasty to princely rank and reduced another to baronial level was not the rights which all shared but the power to make something of those rights; and that power, however many

[27] Cf. particularly *Territorium u. Stadt* (2nd ed.), 1—52, and the summary in *Vom Mittelalter z. Neuzeit*, 22—45.

fortuitous factors might contribute to it, was based in the last resort on a wide demesne and ample resources.[28] Few historians to-day are prepared to seek the source of the late mediaeval principality in any single institution or element. The facts show that what was decisive was precisely a combination, a union, of all the sources of power—county rights, church fiefs, advocacies, allodial lands—and it would be hard, in fact, to find a princely family which failed to draw on all these elements in establishing its position. Jurisdictional rights needed the support of material resources; but material resources alone, though they could make a man rich and powerful, could never make him sovereign, unless they were combined with jurisdictional rights. Rights which were originally rights over persons needed, moreover, to be attached to the soil: they needed " territorialization," and this was most readily achieved where they could be combined with the rights of a landed proprietor[29]—indeed, it can be shown that it was rarely possible to retain either lands which were mere estates or jurisdictional rights lacking a substratum of *Grundherrschaft,* and that the boundaries of the later principalities normally corresponded with the limits of a consolidated authority, to the establishment of which both jurisdictional rights and land ownership had contributed equally.[30]

[28] Thus Knapp, who accepted v. Below's thesis (p. 45) in the words: " Landesherr wurde der Gerichtsherr, dem die hohe und, wo diese geteilt war, die oberste Gerichtsbarkeit zustand, wie denn auch umgekehrt der Verlust der hohen Gerichtsbarkeit den der Landeshoheit herbeiführte," finally modified it incisively (p. 78), when he stated that " blood justice " or supreme criminal jurisdiction, although it conferred an expectation of sovereignty, was not sufficient in itself, unless the territorial lord were otherwise strong enough to acquire or exercise the other functions of a ruler. As soon as the element of strength is admitted, however, the question of material resources becomes predominant. Cf. also v. Schwerin, *Grundzüge d. deutschen Rechtsgesch.*, 173—174.

[29] Klewitz, 18.

[30] Klewitz, 27, 30, 35—37; similarly Spindler, 143.

We can, however, not only postulate that a fusion of rights and powers of various origins was the real source of the *Landeshoheit*, but can show also how that fusion came about. It was achieved by the creation of a new administrative unit, the castellany or *Burgbezirk*, which is found all over Germany, in the Saxon north[31] and the Bavarian south,[32] in ecclesiastical principalities[33] and on the crown lands of the Hohenstaufen.[34] And the castellan himself, as in other parts of Europe,[35] was much more than a mere military officer, whose functions were confined to the castle or fortified town in which he was stationed.[36] His *Burg* was the middle point of an administrative district,[37] in which he exercised jurisdiction: it was the centre from which the authority of the prince was exerted and in a large degree the foundation on which that authority was constructed.[38] Built where possible on allodial land and the centre of a demesne, the castle was not only a means by which the demesne lands could be more rigorously administered, but also a fixed point in

[31] Hildebrand, 387.

[32] Spindler, 143—144.

[33] Klewitz, 29—37.

[34] Niese, 222 sqq. (" Burgen und Burgenverfassungen "); Klewitz, *Gesch. d. Ministerialität im Elsass* (1929), 57; Weller, *Württ. Vierteljahrshefte* XXXVI, 158.

[35] Cf. for example, Powicke, *Loss of Normandy*, 35, 38, 42—43, 271, and Mitteis, *Lr. u. Sg.*, 289, 355.

[36] Cf. K. A. Eckhardt, " Präfekt u. Burggraf," ZRG. *Germ. Abt.* XLVI (1926), 163—205.

[37] H. v. Voltelini, " Die Entstehung d. Landgerichte," *Arch. f. österr. Gesch.* XCIV (1907), 25 sqq.

[38] Spindler, 143, modifies—without denying—the significance of the *Burgbezirk* and the validity of the theory that the castle was the centre of the new administration; for, he says, the theory " setzt den Burgbezirk als das zeitlich Frühere an; hier aber liegen Burgenbau und Gerichtsbildung nicht weit auseinander, wenn sie nicht überhaupt zusammenfallen." I cannot, however, see how this fact, if we may take it for proved, invalidates the theory, for *Burgenbau* and *Gerichtsbildung* are essentially two sides of one and the same process, the object of which is a general reorganisation of administration. Except where a conveniently situated castle already existed, we should expect simultaneous introduction.

which governmental rights could be concentrated. Attached in this way to a territorial centre, the rights of jurisdiction vested in the prince could be " territorialized ",[39] attached to consolidated territorial districts and used as a means of uniform government. Such is the basis of the princely government of the later middle ages; and though all sorts of rights and powers may have been incorporated in the *Burgbezirke* and *districtus* of the growing states, what really establishes those states on a firm foundation is the capacity to develop, in the later years of the twelfth century, a new form of administration. Without this reorganization the principalities could not have come into existence.

What matters, therefore, is the creative power, so vigorous in the twelfth century, which resulted in a new undifferentiated administrative organization that had cast off all traces of its origins, and in face of this decisive event, it is of small significance to be able to point to the undoubted fact that one element in the new organization was the jurisdiction vested in the count of earlier centuries. This is not the jurisdiction which the prince is exercising in his *terra* at the end of the thirteenth century.[40] It must be remembered, in the first place, that the supreme

[39] Klewitz, *Hildesheim*, 31: " Die Burgen werden die Zentren, von denen aus diese Herrschaft geübt wird. Von ihnen aus wird eine straffe Verwaltung des kirchlichen Grundbesitzes möglich, und indem zugleich Hoheitsrechte an diese Burgen gezogen werden, gelingt es, diese Rechte zu territorialisieren, so sehr, dass sie auch Geltung erlangen über ein Gebiet, mit dem sie ursprünglich nichts zu tun hatten." We are therefore justified in regarding *Burgenpolitik* as " den folgenschwersten Schritt zur endgültigen Landesherrschaft."

[40] " Das Recht, den Hochrichter einzusetzen . . . und die Durchführung des mittelalterlichen Standrechtes, die Verfolgung der landschädlichen Leute, gehen über den Umfang der gräflichen Gerichtsrechte wesentlich hinaus;" Hirsch, HG. 208 (cf. also p. 238).—The exaggeration of v. Below's thesis, that each function or attribute of the territorial prince, with the exception of direct taxation (*Bede, Steuer*), can be traced back to the count, is particularly apparent when he presents an authoritative summary of his doctrine in his book, *Vom Mittelalter z. Neuzeit*, 34—38.

criminal jurisdiction which was an essential element
of the sovereignty of the princes only came to the
fore with the growth of the " peace movement " in
the twelfth century:[41] the transformation of criminal
jurisdiction between the reigns of Henry IV and
Frederick I was so radical that any continuity which
existed with an earlier age was more apparent than
real—to emphasize it is to lose sight of the essentially
new significance which the twelfth century attached
to criminal jurisdiction and of the novel consequences
which were drawn from its exercise.   As a source of
princely power, therefore, *haute justice* was in essence
a new factor.[42]   The same is true of the right of
" devolution," the right to resume *bona vacantia*,
which has often been regarded as the revival of an
ancient tribal custom.[43]   The novelty of the principle
of direct taxation, on the other hand, of the *Stiura*,
Steuer or *Bede*, is admitted by all historians;[44] and
VON BELOW himself concedes that regalian rights
such as safe-conduct, imposition of customs duties,
the mining monopoly and market rights, were never
a part of the ordinary attributes of the count.[45]
Thus none of the really significant rights or prerogatives on which the sovereignty of the princes was
built was derived from the earlier count, any more
than their territories were simple agglomerations of
ancient counties.

The whole theory of the origin of the principality
in the county is, in fact, based on an exaggeration
and misunderstanding not merely of the strength
and durability of the Frankish county organization,

[41] Hirsch, HG., 221, 226, 229, etc.
[42] *Ibid.*, 222.
[43] Cf. Spindler, 95—99.
[44] The literature (particularly v. Below and Waas) is surveyed by
Spindler, 125 sqq.
[45] *Vom Mittelalter z. Neuzeit*, 38.

but also of its original character. It presupposes an exclusive network of counties in which all freemen were comprised, a comprehensive jurisdiction exercised by royal officials alone. But not even Charles the Great—unlikely though it is that he ever entertained such a project—could realize a programme so comprehensive as this. From the very beginning the county was only one form of judicial and administrative organization, existing side by side with others, more deeply rooted, more ancient and more hardy. It was only one form among many because in Germany there was never the *tabula rasa* on which central authority could build unimpeded, the sweeping away of old institutions which the anarchy of the ninth and tenth centuries produced in France and which the Norman Conquest may perhaps to some extent have created in England. The persistence of allodial land in Germany is well known and constitutionally very significant—it is no accident, for example, that the castles of the eleventh and twelfth centuries are built almost exclusively on allodial land[46]—but less well known and less widely accepted is the existence of "allodial", "autogenous" or "immune" jurisdiction. Few historians to-day, however, would deny this fact.[47] To understand it, we must understand the social organization of the Frankish people, particularly the division of the class of freemen into small peasant proprietors, on the one hand, and into a close but

[46] Hirsch, HG., 142.

[47] Cf. *infra* II, 15—17 (where the older literature is cited), and p. 214 sq.; cf. also E. F. Otto's recent volume, *Adel u. Freiheit* (1937), I. v, particularly pp. 188—191.—The term "autogenous" (autocthonous"), which is used here because it may be said to have been accepted as a *terminus technicus*, is due to Aubin, whose particular merit it is to have traced the existence of jurisdictions or liberties not derived from the crown, but of independent "indigenous" origin.

mighty aristocracy which appears in contemporary
records as the class of *potentes*.[48] The charters
reveal an equality between *potentes* and *comites*, on
the one hand, and between *potentes* and *episcopi et
abbates*, on the other.[49] Their privileged position
has been hidden because only those laymen who were
not *potentes* needed a formal grant from the king
in order to enjoy the rights of " immunity ", and
such a grant was rarely made. But it is clear that
the " immunity " conferred on churches and monasteries in Carolingian times was not a privilege which
raised them above the lay nobility, but rather a
privilege which set them on an equality with the
privileged laity. Ecclesiastical immunity, in short,
was modelled on pre-existing secular immunity,
and this immunity was the prerogative of the small
but powerful group of *potentes*, in whose hands the
government of the land lay.[50] Even in Merovingian
times it was specifically provided that the counts
must be chosen from the ranks of the " magnates ",[51]
and there is no evidence that, born to the exercise
of jurisdiction, the latter ever lost their prerogative.
Clothar II's edict shows that the monarchy with
its county organization, far from creating a bureaucracy or a *noblesse de service*, was only chaining the
existing owners of jurisdiction to the crown; but
it never succeeded in making the exercise of jurisdiction the monopoly of those *potentes* who were
chosen to be *comites*.[52] Jurisdictional rights—not
merely the jurisdiction over servile dependents

---

[48] These facts are clearly explained by v. Dungern, *infra* II, 205 sqq.
[49] Dopsch, *Verf.-u. Wirtschaftsgesch.*, 45—50. Cf. E. Mayer, ZRG.
Germ. Abt. XLVI (1926), 457—460.
[50] Cf. *infra* II, 16, 152, 207.
[51] Dopsch, 49.
[52] Philippi, " Alter deutscher Adel u. Herrenstand," *Deutsche Litera-
turzeitung* XXXVIII (1917), 260.

which every freeman possessed, but a jurisdiction over the free peasantry such as the counts exercised on behalf of the crown—remained in aristocratic hands. The classic example is the story which the chroniclers tell of the forbear of the Welfs in the ninth century, of Eticho and his son Henry, and of the father's refusal to countenance any tie of vassalage by which the free *principatus* which the family had exercised from time immemorial might be damaged or transformed into a franchise held from the crown: they were, in short, the equals and not the inferiors of the counts, and the maintenance of this equality was for them as precious as their life blood.[53]   And if few of the *potentes* maintained this attitude of stalwart independence, if few could resist the prospect, as royal officials, of exercising over wider areas the lucrative jurisdictional rights which were theirs *sui iuris* in their own *principatus*, it was still an open question whether the county would be regarded as an appanage to the *principatus* or whether the crown would be able to subordinate the indigenous powers of the " dynasts " to the rights which they exercised as counts.[54]   In fact,

---

[53] *Hist. Welf. Weingarten.*, c. 4 (MG. *Script.* XXI, 459): " Hic itaque Heinricus, cum ad militares annos pervenisset et sue voluntatis compos fieret, ignorante patre ad imperatorem se contulit. Cumque illi summa familiaritate sociaretur . . . tandem consilio principum et maxime ipsius imperatoris instinctu hominium ei et subiectionem fecit, et in beneficio quatuor milia mansuum in superioribus partibus Baioarie ab eo suscepit. Quod cum pater eius percepisset, ratus nobilitatem suam et libertatem nimis esse declinatam, ultra quam credi possit consternatus animo, dolorem suum omnibus caris suis exposuit . . . " and went away into the mountains, " regalibus edificiis et possessionibus ditissimis relictis." The same story— " Eticho vel Welfus erat egregii libertatis princeps, qui nunquam alicui, nec ipsi imperatori, pro aliquo beneficio se subdidit dominio "—appears apparently independently in the *Annalista Saxo* (MG. *Script.* VI, 764), embellished with the story of Henry's feat of ploughing, which brought him not only his 4,000 " mansus " but also the name: Henry of the Golden Plough.—Cf. v. Dungern, *infra* II, 229; E. Mayer, *op. cit.*, 460; H. G. Gengler, *Beiträge z. Rechtsgesch. Bayerns* I (1889), 124–5; Spindler, 120 n. 1.

[54] Gengler I, 146.

the allodial or "autogenous" element proved the stronger. When the "dynasts" built their castles and thus centralized their administration on their allodial lands, they were automatically expressing the fact that the source of their power was not the crown: their official functions were subordinate to their inherent privileges, their counties were appanages of their principalities.[55]

It is no easy task to assess the strength of the "autogenous" powers vested in the narrow class of dynastic *potentes*. Nor is it easy to construct a lucid theory of German constitutional development in which these powers are neither exaggerated nor ignored. But this is a point at which the truth is more important than lucidity and logic. What we may call the "county theory" of the origin of the principalities lacks nothing in lucidity and logic; but it is not comprehensive or impartial enough to cover all the facts of the situation. There was more in the development of the German principalities than the gradual loosening of the ties which bound both counts and counties to the crown. Throughout Europe the tendency to a dissolution of the bonds on which government was based, was perennial. But in Germany it was reinforced by a spirit of independence, which the legend of Eticho the Welf illustrates, and which had a solid constitutional background. "Autogenous" jurisdiction, "autogenous" rights, were deeply embedded in the social structure. The consciousness of a position of authority, not derived from the king, but based on the ancient prerogatives of a privileged class, which either did not exist elsewhere or ceased to exist at an early

[55] Hirsch, HG., 148–9, and MIÖG. XXXV, 68: "Der Burgenbau ist das deutlichste Zeichen, dass an die Stelle des früheren Amtscharakters nun ein erbliches Herrschaftsrecht getreten war."

date, remained alive. No breach of continuity, no general collapse, occurred to disturb the privileges of the German *potentes*. On the other hand, the autogenous rights of the dynastic nobility would not have been in themselves a sufficient basis even to withstand the mighty royal dominion which the Saxon and Salian monarchs had built up. But they were not thrown back on their autogenous rights alone. The narrow aristocratic class had the monopoly, we have seen, of countships and advocacies, even for a time of bishoprics and abbeys:[56] government in all its forms was concentrated in its hands. For this reason it is extremely difficult to analyse the sources of dynastic power or to separate the various roots of the later principality: the one reinforced the other, and what matters, as we have said, is the fusion of all to produce a new unit of government. That this fusion was possible, on the other hand, seems to have been due above all else to the fact that counties and advocacies could be anchored to allodial lands, that the magnate was already exercising *iure suo* rights similar to those which accrued to him as count or advocate.[57] There was, therefore, always a core around which such rights as were derived from the central government could be consolidated, an organization within which they could be comprised. However much the dynasts owed to the rights conferred on them by the crown—and it was undoubtedly much—the strength of their position was their allodial land and their " autogenous " jurisdiction. It was because they had this position to defend that their hostility

[56] Cf. A. Schulte, *Der Adel u. die deutsche Kirche* (2nd ed., 1922), 26, and *Nachtrag*, 31.
[57] Cf. Aubin, *Landeshoheit*, 164 sqq., 169 sqq., 239 sqq., 245 sqq., and Hirsch, HG., 131 sqq., 225 sqq.

to Henry IV was implacable: it was because they
had this unassailable stronghold to fall back on and
to operate from, that they could transform all their
holdings, fragments of counties, fiefs, advocacies,
into consolidated territories. The backbone of the
whole was the allodial demesne, the *freies Eigen.*
As the twelfth and thirteenth centuries proceeded,
much that was new was to be added, proportions
were to change, and new factors were to increase
in importance: there were, as we have seen, many
novel elements, only developed in the twelfth century
or only then imbued with constitutional significance,
which went to make the late mediaeval principality.
But at the time of the Investiture Contest, when the
dynastic aristocracy showed that it was strong
enough to resist the unswerving application of
monarchical principles which the Salians planned to
enforce, the strength of the aristocratic opposition
was its rich allodial properties and its " autogenous "
rights, and after Henry IV's death, when the process
of rebuilding began and Germany was shaped and
redivided by the aristocracy into new administrative
units, the core of the new divisions was allodial land
and the castles built on allodial land. Here the independent power of the dynasts was centred; and
from this centre the new principalities grew.

V

CONSTITUTIONAL PROBLEMS OF THE TWELFTH CENTURY

WHEN we realize the strength and durability of the " autogenous " current in German history, we can understand not only the falsity of a theory of development which takes account of one type of nobility alone, the *noblesse de service* of the countly class, but we can also understand the strength of the opposition which the German monarchy had to face in its attempts to tie all jurisdiction to the crown. If we wish to enumerate the factors which really differentiated German development from that of England or France, therefore, the first in time and in importance is the persistence of a mighty allodial nobility. It is this fact alone which makes clear the overwhelming difficulty of the task which Henry III and Henry IV proposed for themselves. It is not our business to discuss the political causes of the civil wars which broke out at the end of the eleventh century; but it is fair to say that emphasis on the ecclesiastical factor and on the " tribal " opposition in Saxony—an opposition, it should be noted, which Henry IV had already defeated when his greatest difficulties began[1]—has obscured the underlying fact that Salian policy was, above all, an attack on the privileged position of the dynastic aristocracy. Ministerial government threatened the monopoly which the " dynasts " claimed in countships and

[1] Cf. *infra* II, 113.

95

advocacies.[2] The church policy which we have described was an even more direct attack: if the proprietary houses of the " dynasts " were comprised in the one great *Reichskirche*, what guarantee was there for the proprietary rights which the lords who had built the monasteries had no intention of surrendering? What was to prevent the supreme advocate, the king, nominating a stranger as his local agent to exercise his functions?[3] What was to prevent his gradually transforming the advocacy in this way into a temporary charge, held *ex officio* and *ad nutum principis*? It is not surprising that, at a time when internal colonization was enlarging monastic demesnes[4] and the consequent rise in importance of the dependent classes was emphasizing the value of jurisdictional rights,[5] the constitutional struggle of the reigns of Henry IV and Henry V should centre round the advocacy, and that the dynastic aristocracy should insist on its right to exercise without royal licence every form of jurisdiction including supreme jurisdiction in life and limb over the tenants of the monasteries it had founded.[6] If the crown ever intended to reserve jurisdiction in life and limb for itself,[7] such a policy was impossible at a time when it was fighting on two fronts, and when the aristocratic families were exploiting the

[2] *Infra* II, 152.
[3] Waas I, 171.
[4] Cf. Th. Mayer, *infra* II, 182 sqq.; cf. Hirsch, HG., 142.
[5] HG., 230.
[6] *Infra* II, 156.
[7] It has been pointed out that Henry IV's " Vogteiweistümer schweigen von dem Blutgericht des Vogtes und beschränken sich darauf, die ihm gebührenden finanziellen Leistungen festzulegen." But " was sich etwa zur Zeit Heinrichs III. oder in den Jahren, da seine regierungsunfähige Witwe das Steuer führte, noch hätte machen lassen, war nach den Ergebnissen des Investiturstreits schlechterdings undurchführbar. Die Dynasten drangen mit ihren Ansprüchen auf das Hoch- und Blutgericht durch " (HG., 149).

dual struggle to create immunities and *Hochgerichts-bezirke* without royal sanction.[8]   Henry IV came to terms with the papacy in order to deal with the dynasts: Henry V, pursuing the same objects, preferred the opposite method.[9]   To win aristocratic support he had to recognize the *de facto* position which had arisen during the thirty years in which there had been no *rex catholicus*.   But his recognition had limits.   The royal ban, which a century earlier had been no more than the title by which the sub-advocates of the royal proprietary churches exercised their delegate authority,[10] was transformed and applied without limitation to every exercise of high criminal jurisdiction.[11]   If Henry, in short, made far-reaching concessions to the dynasts, the dynasts made equally significant concessions to him, and what he had won was more permanently affirmed in 1149 when the princes acceded to the judgement of the imperial court " quod nullus posset causas vel lites, que ad advocatorum ius pertinerent, audire vel terminare vel placita advocatie tenere, nisi qui bannum de manu regia recepisset."[12]

Even if there is no doubt which party won the more substantial advantage, it is still noteworthy that the crown did not emerge empty-handed from the Investiture Contest.   The recognition of its supremacy implicit in the *Bannleihe* was no empty formula.   And in other ways the crown's position was still full of rich potentialities.   If the new monastic orders of the eleventh century had escaped its control and passed under the advocacy of the dynasts,

[8] *Infra* II, 149—150, and Dopsch, *Verf.-u. Wirtschaftsgesch.*, 68 sq.
[9] Hirsch, HG. 140, 235, and MIÖG. XXXV (1914), 69—72.
[10] HG., 175-6.
[11] *Ibid.*, 177, 179—180, 182—183; cf. Aubin, *Landeshoheit*, 244—246.
[12] MG. *Const.* I, 181 (No. 127).

it was more successful in dealing with the new orders
of the twelfth century, Cistercians and Premon-
stratensians.[13] By the beginning of Barbarossa's
reign it was a generally accepted rule that such
houses " nullum habeant advocatum preter Romanorum imperatorem ", and if—as we shall see—this
rule was subsequently transformed into the very
different principle: " neque advocatum eis habere
liceat, nisi defensorem principem ipsum, qui caput
est terre, in qua quique eorum degunt," it meant
nevertheless that the twelfth century monarchy
profited to the same extent from the remarkable
expansion of the Cistercian order as the dynasts had
profited from that of Hirsau. Nor was its position
in regard to the bishoprics and to the *Reichskirche*
as a whole weakened to the extent which is still
generally maintained. Now that the controversy
about the significance of the Concordat of Worms
has been brought to a brilliant close by ADOLF
HOFMEISTER's conclusive survey of the problem,[14]
we can see that the relations between the crown and
the imperial church in the twelfth century were
constructed, not on specific terms agreed to in 1122,
but on the incomparably broader basis of immemorial
custom. Henry V's charter was, indeed, a final and

[13] Hirsch, Klosterimmunität, cap. IV; cf. H. Zeiss, *Hist. Jahrb.*
XLVI (1926), 594—601.

[14] " Das Wormser Konkordat. Zum Streit um seine Bedeutung,"
*Forschungen u. Versuche z. Gesch. d. Mittelalters u. d. Neuzeit (Festschrift
Dietrich Schäfer,* 1915), 64—148.—It was originally intended to include
a translation of this distinguished essay in the present work, and the author
kindly gave his permission; but it eventually proved impossible to produce
a version which would be fully comprehensible to those not already acquainted with the bulk of controversial literature, without introducing
changes more extensive than could be justified. For this reason the translation which has been prepared, has had to be omitted; but it is hoped
that the brief remarks here made, will call the attention of English historians
to the essay. The short note in the *Cambridge Medieval History* V, 108,
hardly does justice to Prof. Hofmeister's arguments. Cf. Hampe, *Wissen-
schaftliche Forschungsberichte* VII (1922), 69.

unambiguous surrender of the old proprietary bond
between crown and *Reichskirche*; but when this
concession had been made, the papacy—to the extreme dissatisfaction of the prelates assembled in
the Lateran Council of 1123—withdrew its opposition
to the other methods by which the crown maintained
its legitimate influence over the church, and specifically accepted the main points of the royal position
in the charter which Calixtus II granted to Henry V.
Historians have always found it difficult to understand how the crown, which had made a permanent
concession to God and the holy catholic church,
could be satisfied with a temporary concession from
the reigning pope to the reigning emperor;[15] but
the attempts to show that the papal charter, in
spite of its form, was valid in perpetuity having been
undermined by SCHÄFER,[16] it remained for HOF-
MEISTER to prove that the personal form, far from
placing the monarchy at the mercy of the papacy,
had positive advantages.[17]   If the king's rights in

[15] Henry's charter reads: " Ego Heinricus . . . dimitto Deo et sanctis
Dei apostolis Petro et Paulo sancteque catholice ecclesie . . . ", whereas
the papal charter begins: " Ego Calixtus . . . tibi dilecto filio Heinrico
Dei gratia Romanorum imperatori augusto concedo . . .".   The difference
of formulation is obvious, and clearly not accidental.   Cf. the texts in
Eichmann, *Quellensammlung z. kirchl. Rechtsgesch.* I (1925), 27—28.

[16] " Zur Beurteilung des Wormser Konkordats," *Abhandl. d. preuss.
Akademie*, 1905.

[17] The essential basis for this conclusion was a study of the various
documents in which a solution of the issues between church and state
was sought between 1111 and 1122; Hofmeister, 76—81.   Such a comparison revealed the fact that the notorious *pravilegium* of 13 April 1111, which
is well known to have been drafted entirely in accordance with the wishes
of the victorious king, was also a personal concession to the reigning
sovereign.   " How," Hofmeister justifiably asks (p. 77), " is it conceivable
that Henry, at such a moment of victory, was satisfied with a purely personal concession ? "   The answer is that Paschal was only confirming a
right which, created by long usage, already existed without his confirma-
tion: " Illam igitur dignitatis prerogativam, quam predecessores nostri
vestris predecessoribus catholicis imperatoribus concesserunt et privi-
legiorum paginis confirmaverunt, nos quoque dilectioni tuae concedimus
et presentis privilegii pagina confirmamus " (Eichmann, 27).   The solution
which Paschal had proposed in February 1111, on the other hand, the

the church had been based on a papal privilege,
they would have been rights held from the church
and dependent in the last analysis on the good-will
of the pope, for no affirmation of permanence could
prevent one pope taking away what another had
granted. Based instead on the immemorial custom
of the realm, which Calixtus II had recognized and
by recognizing approved, the king's position was
independent and firmly rooted in a long and independent tradition of imperial government.[18] And—
what is more important from our point of view—it
was flexible. Far from being bound by the specific
terms of an unequivocable agreement, the king was
free to act in accordance with a living practice.
There is no doubt that at first the king hoped to
maintain his control of the bishoprics by a strict
exercise of his right to hold elections " in the royal
presence ".[19]   This was the method which the
English monarchy used to perfection;[20] but it proved
impracticable in Germany, and already by 1142 or
1143 Gerhoh of Reichersberg was rejoicing that
elections were no longer being held in court.[21] The
strength of the royal position, however, was soon
apparent; for when its control of elections broke
down, the monarchy was free to emphasize the other
rights which it had retained in 1122.   In the first
place, the king developed the claim to nominate

restoration of *regalia* to the monarchy, implied a revolutionary change,
and was therefore embodied in a charter issued to Henry and his successors
in perpetuum (Eichmann, 25).   Exactly the same distinction, Hofmeister
proves, is to be made between the two charters, papal and imperial, of 1122.

[18] Hofmeister, 94—95, 116—118.

[19] Hofmeister, 88 sqq.   " In praesentia tua " means " in court," as
Hofmeister proves against other interpretations, pp. 91—92.

[20] Hofmeister, 93; cf. *Const. Clar.*, c. 12 (Stubbs, *Select Charters*,
9th ed., 166).

[21] " Illa propter pacem obtinendam extorta concessio partim est
annichilata, quia Deo gratias absque regis presentia fiunt electiones episcoporum " (MG. *Lib. de lite* III, 280); cf. Hofmeister, 105, 109.

whoever he wished in disputed elections.[22] But more important still was the transference of emphasis, apparent from the beginning of Frederick I's reign, from election to the right of investiture.[23] In maintaining that no bishop might dispose of *regalia* unless he had previously been invested by the king, Frederick was expressly building on the *usus approbatus* of the realm and on the *rationes curiae*, the considered practice of the royal court.[24] It would be surprising if usage and practice had not corresponded in some degree with the compromise of 1122; but the vitality and constructive quality of Barbarossa's ecclesiastical policy is due precisely to the fact that it was not based on a specific Concordat, but sprang directly out of the traditions of imperial government. In this sense, all historians are agreed that Frederick I went—as he was entitled to go—beyond the precise terms of the Concordat of Worms and maintained direct contact with earlier law.[25] But a simple revival of the Ottonian *Reichskirche* was an unfeasible as it was inadequate.[26] Apart from the fact that the essential problem in the twelfth century was to define the relationship between the crown and

[22] Hofmeister, 115. This right, which neither Barbarossa nor Henry VI had any difficulty in substantiating, was, of course, totally different from the earlier right to have all elections carried out " in praesentia regis "; cf. Hinschius, *Kirchenrecht* II (1878), 563 sqq.

[23] Hofmeister, 109 sqq.

[24] For explicit reference to the *rationes curiae*, cf. Hofmeister, 115, n. 1. The reference to the *usus approbatus* and the *iusticia imperii* is in a letter of 1186 (MG. *Const.* I, 445) from Wichmann, archbishop of Magdeburg, to Urban III: " videretur inperium demembrationem et maximam sui iuris diminutionem incurrisse, praesertim cum nulli antecessorum suorum ab aliquo antecessorum vestrorum factum fuisse antiquitatis curiosa reportet memoria, quod episcoporum quispiam in regno Teutonico consecrationem prius quam regalia per sceptrum imperiale receperit. Quod quidem rationi non derogans in haec usque tempora usus approbatus celebri firmitate conservavit. Sed nec hanc imperii iusticiam infringendam per vos aut aliquatenus permutandam dominus imperator credidit."

[25] Cf. Hauck, *Kirchengesch.* IV (1913), 198—202; Hinschius, II, 565, 570; Schäfer, 60—63; Hofmeister, 110—111.

[26] Hirsch, HG., 232; cf. *infra* II, 159.

the new forces in the ecclesiastical hierarchy which
the Investiture Contest had created,[27] the old proprietary bond with the *Reichskirche* had gone for
ever. Investiture in the days of Frederick I was a
very different institution from investiture in the
days of Henry III.[28] The essential point was, by
uncompromising insistence on enfeoffment *per sceptrum*, to weld an unbreakable feudal bond between
crown and ecclesiastical prince;[29] and in this policy
Frederick Barbarossa was entirely successful. The
civil wars under Henry IV and Henry V had destroyed the old connexion between church and state:
a new connexion, suited to new circumstances, was
defined in the twelfth century by a monarchy which
was still able to call on the living tradition of
imperial law. The relations of church and state
were feudalized.

Subjection to the rules of feudal law, comprehen-
sion within a strictly organized feudal hierarchy,
was, however, not merely an expedient for regulating
the relations of church and state which the Investiture Contest had convulsed. On the contrary, it
was the principle of reorganization on which the
whole work of the Hohenstaufen was firmly based.
All the great constitutional changes which centre
round the fall of Henry the Lion—the construction
of a limited *Reichsfürstenstand*, the formulation of
the *Heerschild* system—imply the recognition of a
feudal organization as the basis of government.[30]

[27] Hirsch, *Klosterimmunität*, 111.
[28] Cf. A. Scharnagl, *Der Begriff d. Investitur in d. Quellen u. d. Litera-
tur des Investiturstreites* (1908).
[29] Cf. Mitteis, *infra* II, 242 sq.
[30] Cf. in Vol. II the essays by Mitteis and v. Dungern, where these
questions are considered in detail; and cf. also Mayer, *infra* II, 16, 28.
Rosenstock, *Königshaus*, part II, analyses the constitutional revolution
thoroughly, and opens up many new perspectives; and for a very brief
summary, cf. Blondel, *Politique de l'empereur Frédéric*, cap. III, § 1.

This is the basis of relations with the new duchies
which were created in the twelfth century as well
as with the ecclesiastical principalities. And reorganization on feudal lines was beyond all doubt
the policy—perhaps even the conscious and systematic policy—of the monarchy, not a compromise
forced on the crown by a victorious baronage, a
series of concessions which were only made because
they could not be avoided. The rise of the new
duchies—Austria, Steiermark, Würzburg, Westphalia
—is still almost uniformly regarded as a sign of the
decay of royal authority: although it is obvious,
even from a narrow political point of view, that
division of the vast Welf territories was the easiest
way for the crown to maintain predominance over
the whole, the new ducal power is regarded as a force
which rose in opposition to the crown.[31] Against
this view, however, more than one historian has
emphasized the fact that neither hostility nor opposition between crown and princes is at all apparent
during Barbarossa's reign.[32] Barbarossa's relations
with Henry the Lion, it has long been recognized,
were genuinely harmonious for twenty years and
more.[33] The contest with Alexander III revealed
the ecclesiastical princes—very different from their
predecessors under Henry IV and their successors
under Frederick II—in solid unison with their ruler,[34]

[31] For what follows, cf. Hirsch, HG., 210, 236, and MIÖG. XXXV,
75 sqq.
[32] Dopsch, Verf.- u. Wirtschaftsgesch., 78.
[33] Cf. Güterbock, Barbarossa u. Heinrich d. Löwe, 256–7.
[34] Hauck IV, 256–7. The exception was Eberhard of Salzburg; but
even his attitude was " correct " rather than enthusiastic—he appeared,
e.g., at Frederick's court, but refused to attend Alexander's—and Frederick
had consequently no difficulty in tolerating him; cf. Hauck, 260. Subsequently dissatisfaction grew in Lorraine (p. 269) under French influence;
but the Diet of Würzburg restored unity in 1165; cf. Hauck, 277, 280, 283.
Alexander's plan, " in Deutschland eine Revolution zu erregen, wie einst-
mals gegen Heinrich IV," was (says Hauck, 262) a complete failure.

and it would be hard to show that any bishop sought to exploit the antagonism between empire and papacy to gain territorial concessions for himself. But the fact is that—in spite of the ultimate breach with Henry the Lion—nothing was more distant from the minds either of the king or of those princes who, with the definition of the *Reichsfürstenstand*, were to become his tenants-in-chief, than mutual antagonism. Far from struggling between each other for control of sovereign rights, each party was co-operating wholeheartedly in the one great task of restoring governmental authority.

Throughout Europe the twelfth century was marked by a process of reconstruction which was so strong as to merit the name of a constitutional revolution.[35] It was a process uniform in object but varied in method, adapted in each land to the actualities of the constitutional situation. What we have already said—and what is explained in greater detail in the essays which follow[36]—of the "dynastic" class and of its claims and objectives, enables us to understand why, in Germany, reconstruction was achieved through the co-operation of crown and princes. It was the "dynastic" class which had emerged triumphant from the constitutional struggles under Henry IV, and it was with the independence and increased rights of this privileged aristocracy that statesmen in the twelfth century had to cope. But Frederick I could not hope to undertake single-handed and against immeasurably greater odds the task which had overwhelmed Henry IV. An intermediate authority, which would carry out the subjection of the "dynasts" in the sense of the crown and which would

---

[35] Cf. particularly Brackmann, *infra* II, 281—299.

[36] *Infra* II, 15, 27, 29, 152—153, 166—167, 169—173, 185, 192, 205—209, 214, 227—230.

be directly interested in carrying out such a policy was necessary, and this intermediate authority was created by the formation of the new duchies. More intense economic life, the work of colonization, internal and external, which played so large a part in the transformation of mediaeval Germany,[37] the growing importance of the dependent classes with whom the central government of Ottonian times had had no direct contact, worked in the same direction, for the new tasks and functions which economic and social change imposed on government necessitated the introduction of a more complicated administrative organization in which intermediate powers could help in the task of controlling the dynastic counts and advocates. Consciousness of this necessity is apparent, very notably, in the famous provision of the privilege which accompanied the creation of the Austrian duchy in 1156: "statuimus quoque, ne aliqua magna vel parva persona in eiusdem ducatus regimine sine ducis consensu vel permissione aliquam iusticiam presumat exercere."[38] The essence of this provision is not, as is still usually supposed, a transference of royal rights to the new duke or an undertaking by the crown to refrain from intervention in the jurisdiction of the duchy, but an authorization to subject the dynastic aristocracy and the criminal jurisdiction of which it had got possession, to governmental authority. It was, in short, not at the expense of the crown but at the expense of the " dynasts " that the duchy or *principatus* was built up and consoli-

[37] Cf. Th. Mayer, *infra* II, 17—26, 191—193.

[38] MG. *Const.* I, 222 (No. 159). There is a similar provision in the privilege of 1168 for Würzburg: " decernentes, ne aliqua ecclesiastica secularisve persona ... per totum Wirziburgensem episcopatum et ducatum et cometias infra terminos episcopatus vel ducatus sitas iudiciariam potestatem ... deinceps exerceat, nisi solus Wirzeburgensis episcopus et dux, vel cui ipse commiserit."

dated.[39]   And the same fact can be seen in other
connexions.   If the general rule that Cistercian houses
should have no *Vogt* except the emperor himself was
soon altered to include the *princeps terre*,[40] the
immediate result was that the numerous founders
of Cistercian houses, unlike the founders of reformed
monasteries a century earlier, were unable to make
their foundations a basis of dominion by retaining
jurisdiction over the monastic lands in their own
hands.[41]   The aristocracy which had profited by the
Hirsau movement to strengthen its constitutional
position found itself cut off from the profits of Cistercian expansion, which passed instead into the
coffers of Hohenstaufen, Wittelsbach, Babenberg,
and Habsburg.   This fundamental contrast with the
eleventh century is typical.   The constitutional
progress achieved in the twelfth century can be
summed up very simply as the defeat of the dynastic
power which had emerged triumphant in 1105; and
the immediate fruits of the victory, which was the
result of loyal co-operation between the crown and
the new princely class, were shared among the
victors.   This is true under Barbarossa and Henry VI
and remains true under Frederick II.   But the
" dynasts " were tenacious of their rights and privileges, and the struggle was long and bitter.   Only
the end of the thirteenth or the beginning of the
fourteenth century saw the completion of the first
phase of territorial reconstruction, and by that time
only one of the twelfth-century partners was left.
The Hohenstaufen had disappeared from the scene,

[39] Cf. particularly Hirsch, MIÖG. XXXV (1914), 82 sqq.—The whole
paragraph, it should be acknowledged, is built up on his compelling arguments, which have found general acceptance; cf. Dopsch, *Verf.- u. Wirtschaftsgesch.*, 77 sqq.
[40] *Supra*, 98.
[41] Hirsch, *Klosterimmunität*, 134.

and the princes alone were able to book the profits resulting from the policy which Barbarossa had inaugurated.

For those who regard the constitutional reorganization of the twelfth century as the establishment of consolidated principalities in competition with the crown, it is easy to say that the ultimate failure of the Hohenstaufen to retain their hold was implicit in the policy adopted by Barbarossa. We have tried, on the other hand, to show that the consolidation of the principalities was begun at the expense not of the crown but of the independent dynastic aristocracy, just as we have tried—by explaining the privileged position of this aristocracy—to show how sound and realistic Barbarossa's policy was. It is easy to decry a policy which demands loyalty and co-operation, especially if it demands the co-operation of a man like Henry the Lion, whose utter incapacity to share high political ideals, whose stolid realism and grasping materialism were as striking to contemporaries as to later generations.[42] But there is no better proof of the solid basis on which Barbarossa's policy was based than the career of Henry the Lion himself. For him the emperor's attitude meant everything. As long as he had Frederick's support his work of building up a north German state by suppressing and subjecting the local powers went from success to success; but when the emperor's backing was withdrawn not even the unsurpassed network of foreign alliances which he had built up as a second line of defence,[43] could save him from the onslaught of the Saxon counts. Even in 1180, after an attack which had lasted a

[42] Cf. for example, infra II, 295.
[43] Cf. R. Schmidt, " Heinrich der Löwe. Seine Stellung in der inneren u. auswärtigen Politik Deutschlands," HZ. CLIV (1936), 241—284.

generation, the dynasts were stronger than Henry the Lion.[44] This was why the monarchy could be sure of the genuine co-operation and loyalty of the new ducal or princely power it had created and enlisted. The princes' energies were absorbed in the struggle with the dynastic aristocracy which the civil war of Henry IV's reign had left firmly entrenched in a position of preponderating might, and which the opening up of new land by reclamation and settlement was likely, if not immediately controlled, to make impregnable.[45] For a struggle with the crown they had neither time nor interest nor desire. Nothing is more clear than the willingness of the new dukes to accept a position under the crown and to acknowledge the royal supremacy which alone could save them from the fate of Henry the Lion. We have seen the lay princes accept the principle: no jurisdiction without the royal ban,[46] and we have seen the ecclesiastical princes, led by Wichmann of Magdeburg, support the emperor in his policy of making enfeoffment *per sceptrum* the essential preliminary to the exercise of episcopal power.[47] It is only necessary to examine the sentences promulgated in the royal court with the assent of the princes to multiply such cases: the constitutions of the realm are the best evidence that there was, among the princes, no thought of denying the sovereign rights of the crown and no conception of a princely power free from the supreme control of the monarch.[48]

[44] Güterbock, 255–6; Hirsch, MIÖG. XXXV, 86; cf. Hildebrand, 376—378, 389—390.
[45] For the constitutional significance of reclamation and colonization, cf. *infra* II, 192.
[46] *Supra*, 97.
[47] *Supra*, 101.
[48] HG., 236–7.

When we understand the co-operation of crown and princes—in the new sense of the term *princeps* which was evolved during Frederick Barbarossa's reign[49]— we can understand also the basis of the new Germany which the Hohenstaufen were building. It cannot, indeed, any more than in England or even in France, be reduced to a simple formula: feudalism or anti-feudalism, centralization or decentralization. There is a very marked tendency to centralization, as there must always be where a process of re-building is at work; but there is decentralization, in so far as much of the re-building is left to the new princely power. As far as the relations of crown and princes are concerned, it is to be a state held together by feudal bonds. Like the France with which Frederick I was acquainted, the France of Louis VII, it was to be a series of duchies grouped round the royal demesne. As in France feudal bonds were to hold the federation together, and just as the reconstitution of state authority by the French dukes ultimately played, by a process of " concentration concentrique," into the hands of Philip Augustus,[50] so without doubt Frederick Barbarossa and his son, who were both consciously influenced not only by Sicilian but also by Capetian and Plantagenet example and well able to compare their own position with that of other monarchs,[51] realized that, unless unforeseen circumstances intervened, every reinforcement of government, whether due to Welfs, Zähringer, Wittelsbach or Babenberger, must ultimately mean a reinforce-

---

[49] For the two senses of the term *princeps* and the definition of the new estate of princes in or about 1180, cf. *infra* II, 16, 229, 250 sqq. Cf. also R. Moeller, " Die Neuordnung des Reichsfürstenstandes u. der Prozess Heinrichs des Löwen," ZRG. *Germ. Abt.* XXXIX (1918), 1—44.

[50] Cf. for example *Lr. u. Sg.*, 282—283.

[51] Cf. Perels, *Erbreichsplan*, 65.—Both Otto of Freising and Rainald of Dassel had studied in France; cf. *infra* II, 249.

ment of the pivot around which the whole of government revolved. It was enough for them to take the
first step: to strengthen government whatever its
form, to revivify the principle of the state. More
than this the Capetians had not, during Barbarossa's
lifetime, achieved. But just as the foundations laid
by Louis VI and Louis VII were the essential basis
for Philip Augustus' successes, so Germany, if placed
on the same foundations as twelfth century France,
might be consolidated round the throne. And if
feudal bonds were a sufficiently potent force to hold
the counts of Flanders and Champagne or the dukes
of Burgundy and Aquitaine in dependence on the
Capetian king, feudal bonds might be relied on to
secure the loyalty of the dukes of Bavaria, Austria
or Saxony to the Hohenstaufen. Although Henry
the Lion was tried both by the common law of the
land and by feudal law, it was the feudal proceedings
which brought him to nothing[52]—the application of
the same principle of feudal justice which enabled
Philip Augustus to triumph over King John.[53]
And even if the political results of the two trials were
strikingly different, even though the Hohenstaufen
were unable, like the Capetians, to incorporate the
escheated lands into the royal demesne,[54] the fall
of Henry the Lion is still clear evidence that feudal
bonds were far from nugatory and provided a reliable
means of holding the state together. The reliance
of the Hohenstaufen on the centralizing force of
feudalism, in short, was not misplaced. But feudalism was no more their sole resource than it was the
sole resource of the kings of France and England.[55]

[52] Mitteis, *infra* II, 249; cf. *Pol. Prozesse*, 72—73.
[53] Mitteis, *Pol. Prozesse*, 114.
[54] *Ibid.*, 115 sqq.
[55] *Infra* II, 261 sqq.

In Germany, as elsewhere in Europe, the monarchy always had its non-feudal capacity, the sovereign was always more than suzerain; and it is one of the particularly instructive aspects of his relations with the church—and one reason why we have not failed to deal with them at some length[56]—to see how successfully he could bring to bear his monarchical prerogatives. Nevertheless it is easy to see that in the long run it is the king's ability to maintain his position at the head of the feudal hierarchy which can alone enable him to make full use of his non-feudal rights. He must be *primus inter pares* if he is successfully to insist on being more than *primus inter pares*. The preservation of his sovereign rights is the factor which raises the king head and shoulders above the other princes, the basis on which, with an adequate material backing, he will be able to transform his feudal overlordship into non-feudal sovereignty. But adequate material backing is necessary: without that, sovereign rights will be empty claims, the king will have the trappings but not the reality of royalty.

As in France, therefore, success depends, in the last analysis, on a sound " demesne policy ". Behind all else, the key which explains every other factor in Hohenstaufen policy, is the endeavour to build up, within the greater realm over which the emperors were set as supreme rulers, a smaller more compact " state " of which they were the sole and immediate lords, governing through a well-organized bureaucracy and exercising a strict centralized control. This Hohenstaufen " state " was no different in kind from the principalities which the new dukes were simultaneously creating in other regions of

[56] *Supra,* 97 sqq.

Germany.[57]   It had a similar organization, was
guided by a similar policy, followed the same objectives.   We can no more stop to follow the detail
of its growth than we can follow in detail the political
measures by which Henry the Lion rounded off his
territory in Saxony or the Wittelsbachs overcame
aristocratic opposition in Bavaria. Economically
and socially, Hohenstaufen policy was guided by the
principles which, as THEODOR MAYER has brilliantly
shown, were adopted by the dukes of Zähringen.
But if the history of the Zähringer " state " can
rightly be selected—where one example has to serve
for many—as the most lucid and characteristic
illustration of the formation and growth of the new
territorial states,[58] there are nevertheless special
reasons why a few words should be said about the
territorial policy of the Hohenstaufen.   Having
sketched the broad outlines of Hohenstaufen constitutional policy, therefore, our next concern must
be the " state " on which the realization of that
policy ultimately depended.

[57] Hildebrand (p. 427, etc.) tries to contrast Henry the Lion's "modern"
and " rationalistic " principles of government with the imperial government
as conceived by Barbarossa; but Güterbock rightly insists that in territorial policy, administration and constitutional outlook, the two were
pursuing exactly similar objectives; cf. Güterbock, *Vergangenheit u.
Gegenwart* XXIII (1933), 260.
[58] *Infra* II, 175—202.

VI

THE HOHENSTAUFEN STATE

A SHORT survey of the territorial policy[1] of the twelfth-century rulers is necessary, in the first place, because the Hohenstaufen " state " was intended to be—though it never became—the core of the new Germany. In this regard the Hohenstaufen had, in the possession of Franconia, the central German land, an undeniable advantage over all other princes.[2] And it was an advantage which they knew how to put to good use. Already before 1158 Barbarossa had acquired the *terra Pliznensis*[3]—a consolidated province bordering on Thuringia and the mark of Meissen[4]—and the Egerland, a similar territory in the same district, had come into Frederick's hands on his marriage with Adela of Vohburg.[5] The frequency with which Frederick held his court at Altenburg, the chief town of the Pleissnerland, is evidence of the importance he attached to the district.[6] And on the death without direct male heirs of the landgrave of Thuringia in 1191 and of the margrave of

---

[1] The essential basis for all further study is H. Niese, *Die Verwaltung des Reichsgutes im* 13. *Jahrhundert* (1905). Cf. further A. Meister, *Die Hohenstaufen im Elsass* (1890); F. Schneider, " Kaiser Friedrich II. u. seine Bedeutung f. d. Elsass," *Elsass-Lothr. Jahrb.* IX (1930), 128—155, and *Kaiser Friedrich II. u. der Staat* (1930); H. W. Klewitz, *Gesch. d. Ministerialität im Elsass* (1929); K. Weller, " Die staufische Städtegründung in Schwaben," *Württ. Vierteljahrshefte f. Landesgesch.* XXXVI (1930), 145—268, and " Zur Organisation d. Reichsgutes in d. späteren Stauferzeit," *Festschr. D. Schäfer* (1915); E. Rosenstock, " Über ' Reich ', ' Staat ' u. ' Stadt ' in Deutschland von 1230—1235," MIÖG. XLIV (1930), 401—416.
[2] Cf. Schmeidler, *infra* II, 82 sqq.
[3] Niese, *Verwaltung*, 44, and HZ. CXII (1914), 555.
[4] Niese, *Verwaltung*, 263 sqq.
[5] *Ibid.*, 10, 11, 15, 266.
[6] *Infra* II, 91.

Meissen in 1195, there is no doubt that Henry VI's
first object was to absorb the vacant fiefs and secure
predominance in the whole of central Germany.
The Franconian lands were, in short, to be the centre
from which, when occasion arose, the crown could
stretch out and add new blocks to its territories.
Such a policy of *arrondissement* was, of course,
shared equally by the princes; and the last years
of his life saw Frederick, for example, engaged in
a hard but successful struggle with the dukes of
Bavaria and Bohemia, the Babenberger and a number
of local counts, for the control of Regensburg—
another key-position between north and south.[7]
But if this policy is a well-known feature of German
political life in the middle ages, it is still too often
supposed that it was a policy which denoted a break
up of royal power, a tendency which could only
result in loss to the crown. Historians still speak
as though the Hohenstaufen were the givers, the
princes the receivers.[8] The fact is that Barbarossa's
territorial policy was a model for the princes: what
the emperor did in Swabia, Henry the Lion applied
in Saxony.[9] Here again, therefore, the policy of the
Hohenstaufen demands special consideration: they
were, as we should expect, leaders in territorial
reorganization.

Franconia and central Germany was one centre of
their power: another was Swabia—where, however,
they shared predominance with the Zähringer—and
special importance attaches to Alsace. From the
great Alsatian palace, Hagenau, in the west to
Altenburg in the east, across the Rhine, through the

---

[7] Spindler, 63—65. It seems that the *Burggrafschaft*, which gave
control of the city, escheated to the crown as a vacant fief; *ibid.*, 17.
[8] Cf. Thompson, 357.
[9] Spindler, 15—16, 94.

upper valleys of Danube and Neckar to the Main
and along the upper reaches of the Main towards
Eger and Elbe, north to Goslar and south to Ulm,
stretched the royal territory. It was not, of course,
any more than the lands of Welf or Wittelsbach, a
consolidated demesne, uniformly dependent on its
royal master. But it could be made into such a
territory, and this the Hohenstaufen set out to do.
Rights and lands are exchanged, county families
are bought out. Above all else the crown sets out
definitely to bring all sovereign rights under its own
control.[10] The monastery of St. Faith, for example,
holds half the jurisdiction in Schlettstadt: in 1217
the king exchanges these rights for his lands and
servile dependents in Schlettstadt, Brunner and
Königsheim. In other words, he surrenders the rights
of a landlord in exchange for the rights of a prince.
Such a policy, repeated a hundred times and more,
will make him sovereign prince, the sole source of
jurisdiction, the sole fount of rights. And as jurisdiction in this way passes to the crown, it is reorgan-
ized and placed in the hands of dependable servants,
who exercise it not as a fief but as an office in the
king's name. The earliest office is that of *advocatus*[11]
—in origin the office of the reeve or bailiff administer-
ing royal demesne; but partly because it tends to

[10] Niese, 56 (whence the example is taken). Schneider, *Elsass*, 143,
sums up with the words: " Er gab grundherrliche Rechte gegen den
Erwerb landesherrlicher hin."
[11] This *Vogtei* has, of course, to be carefully distinguished from the
advocacy over church lands, which we have already discussed: there has
been confusion, e.g., in the case of Zürich (Niese, 72, 182).—What follows
is based on Niese, 168—209, where, however, we are presented—in spite
of repeated indications that the author had grasped the trend of historical
development—with an analysis of the offices of *Schultheiss, Burggraf* and
Vogt (in that order), instead of a reasoned survey and explanation of the
development of the later offices in place of the original *Vogt*. Such development, though complicated and difficult to follow, is nevertheless clear
beyond doubt—cf. Klewitz, *Ministerialität*, 62—although finally, as Niese
remarks (p. 204), all three offices stand on the same level.

become a fief, partly because of the growing scope of administration, particularly the development of urban life, it gives way in the earlier years of Frederick II's reign in many localities to a more modern organization in which *Schultheiss* and *Burggraf* take the place of *Vogt*. This is the organization we have already discussed—the organization of castellanies and *Landgerichte*.[12] Where there is a castle and castellan, judicial and administrative powers are vested in him: elsewhere administration is centred in a village or market-town and placed in the hands of a *Schultheiss*. Sometimes, on the other hand, the *Schultheiss* is the representative (perhaps elected) of the townsfolk, exercising a local jurisdiction over them under the *Burggraf* who is responsible to the king for the town and the surrounding district: sometimes, as at Ulm, this tendency seems to be carried further and two separate administrations are developed, one for town and one for country.[13] Characteristic of the whole organization, in every case, is the administrative dependence of the countryside on the castle or township. Castles and towns are the seats of administration; and the policy of government is to divide the country into approximately equal districts round the chief urban centres. Thus a series of uniform *districtus* was formed, and for the first time there was a possibility of a uniform bureaucratic government, each *officium* or *Amt* working as a properly co-ordinated part of the whole. It is, therefore, not surprising that administrative reorganization brought with it the introduction of direct taxation, assessed on the " office " as such and not on the villages or individuals which composed

[12] *Supra*, 85 sqq.
[13] E.g., Niese, 202.

it.[14] And the efficiency of the new administration was increased by the introduction of a larger unit, the *procuratio* or province. The government of Alsace was in this way centralized in Hagenau;[15] and other provinces were Swabia itself, the Middle Rhine, the Lower Rhine, the Wetterau, the Speyergau and Nürnberg.[16] How successful this organization was is shown by its application in 1237 and 1246 to Austria and Styria, when the two duchies were united to the crown and placed under an official with the title: *per Austriam et Styriam capitaneus procurator*.[17] Nor is there any reason to think that the union of 1246, which lasted until Frederick's death, was intended to be other than permanent.[18] The administration was, in short, so sound and firmly established that it could already absorb new provinces, and the policy of " concentration concentrique " which we have already described[19] was justifying itself as fully in the hands of the Hohenstaufen as it had already justified itself in the hands of the Capetians. The absorption of Austria and Styria, if it had been permanent, would have been an achievement in every way as remarkable as the annexation of Normandy to the crown-lands of France.

Nor did the Hohenstaufen, in their policy of administrative reorganization, neglect the development of their territory and its resources. Like the Zähringer and other princes, they realized the possibilities inherent in the reclamation and cultivation

[14] Cf. Niese, 111, where the connexion is very patent.
[15] Niese, 273–8 ; Schneider, 144.
[16] The provincial organisation is surveyed by Niese, 267—288; cf. also Weller, *Städtegründung*, 160.
[17] Cf. Niese, 286–7.
[18] *Ibid.*, 42—43; cf. Spindler, 189.
[19] *Supra*, 109; cf. Weller, 152.

of the waste and forest which covered so much—
compared with England or France—of early mediaeval Germany.[20] If they placed themselves at the
head of the economic movement for internal colonization, they were concerned not merely to increase their
material resources but also to obtain direct political
control of large tracts of new country which they
could rule on modern principles without the competition of long-existing concurrent authorities. Such
is the significance of the associations of " free peasants ", which are found in increasing numbers from
the twelfth century onwards.[21] It is on the newly
cultivated land that they are found, and their " freedom "—a freedom which was characteristic of the
land and not of the inhabitants, who were servile
colonists and not the remnants of the free peasantry
of Carolingian times—consisted in direct dependence
on the territorial government.[22] They were, in short,
free from intermediate authorities, and attached
directly to the *Landgerichte* which were the new
units of administration. Their " freedom " meant,
in other words, an addition to the power of government: it was a concession by which the territorial
authority extended its direct sphere of influence and
increased the number of inhabitants who looked
directly to the prince to maintain their rights. It
was not everywhere that the new " states " had
recourse to this policy to strengthen their position:
the Zähringer, for example, managed to get full

[20] It is the particular merit of Th. Mayer (*infra* II, 19 sqq.) to have
emphasized for the first time the constitutional significance of internal
colonization.

[21] Cf. K. Weller, " Die freien Bauern in Schwaben," ZRG. *Germ. Abt.*
LIV (1934), 178—226, and Th. Mayer, " Die Entstehung des ' modernen '
Staates im Mittelalter u. die freien Bauern," *ibid.* LVII (1937), 210—288.

[22] It is therefore closely parallel, as Mayer points out (p. 286), to the
libertas which a church or monastery obtained in the eleventh century
through incorporation into the *Reichskirche*; cf. Hirsch, *infra* II, 135-6.

command of advocacies and other jurisdictional rights in the Black Forest at so early a date that it would have been impolitic for them to loosen the bonds which already bound the population by creating a new " free " class.[23] In the Hohenstaufen territory, on the other hand, such rights were still largely in aristocratic hands, and Frederick I and his successors had therefore every reason to throw themselves wholeheartedly into the task of creating a " free peasantry ", which looked to the prince and not to a local lord as its ruler. Their policy was successfully applied in Swabia and later in Switzerland, and was one of the surest means of placing government on a firm territorial foundation.

It is a short step from the " free peasantry " to the towns; for the freedom of the towns was a freedom of exactly the same kind, and the Hohenstaufen sponsored and encouraged urban development for the same reason as they sponsored the development of the new class of " free peasants ". This fact must be emphasized, because it is still a common view that the Hohenstaufen " had no perception of the new economic revolution of the twelfth century."[24] But how, we must ask, could they fail to see the economic importance of the towns, when the account-books of 1241—the discovery of which threw new light on the systematic character of Hohenstaufen finances[25]—show that approximately two-thirds of their revenue was derived, mostly by direct taxation, from urban sources ?[26] And this is only one side of the picture, for, as we have seen, the cities were the

[23] Mayer, *op. cit.*, 216, 288.
[24] Thompson, 358.
[25] The discovery was made by J. Schwalm in 1896; cf. *Neues Archiv* XXIII (1898), 517—553, and K. Zeumer, " Zur Gesch. d. Reichssteuern," HZ. LXXXI (1898), 24—45.
[26] Niese, 114—118.

centres of the new administration, and it is possible to show that the elevation of a township to the rank of borough was accompanied by the displacement of the old official—the *centurio* or hundredman—by the *Schultheiss* or royal reeve, who was the direct representative of his royal master.[27] The Hohenstaufen had therefore the best of reasons for encouraging a town life which was directly dependent on themselves; and their foundations of cities and grants of charters are, in fact, extensive and systematic both in Alsace[28] and in Swabia.[29] The cities with their castles are the " skeleton and backbone " of the land,[30] an essential element in the ministerial organization. Bern, it has been shown, " was essentially a support for the *ministeriales* on the imperial demesnes in Burgundy ", and a similar connexion between ministerial government and city development is evident in such places as Frankfurt, Hagenau and Rotenburg.[31] But the best evidence of the importance attached to the towns by the Hohenstaufen is the famous *Constitutio in favorem principum* of 1232. Regarded as conclusive evidence of the princes' endeavours to emancipate themselves from imperial control, as an attack on the emperor's authority as emperor, it is really a reaction against the " state " which the Hohenstaufen were building up within the greater German state, the crown demesne which was so rapidly becoming a principality.[32] Not

[27] *Ibid.*, 58.

[28] Schneider, 143.

[29] Weller, *Städtegründung*, 169 sqq. (Frederick I's foundations), 187 (Henry VI), 203 sqq. (Frederick II).

[30] Niese, 57; cf. also Weller, 204, who says that for Frederick II the towns were " Grundpfeiler seiner Macht."

[31] Rosenstock, MIÖG. XLIV, 407; Klewitz, 57; and cf. also Weller, 203.

[32] This very important point, conclusively proved by Niese, 52—55, does not seem to have won the recognition which it deserves, though

attack, but defence is its keynote: its contents are
not new princely pretensions but measures dictated
by the fear which the successful demesne policy of
the crown had bred. Already by 1232 the princes
realized that the demesne policy inaugurated by
Barbarossa, if it were not checked, would result in
the absorption, town by town and county by county,
of feudal Germany into the directly governed dominion
of the crown. The situation is revealed, for example,
by the position in Schweinfurt, where the crown held
lands but jurisdiction was vested in the bishop of
Würzburg; but already in 1234 the bishop was
complaining that the royal bailiff was exercising
rights of jurisdiction, and ultimately—in spite of a
temporary concession to the bishop's demands—the
royal *Schultheiss* replaced the episcopal hundredman.[33] Such was the policy which was being pursued
from every royal centre and which was intended
ultimately to give the king a uniform sovereignty
over a consolidated demesne. And of these centres,
the *Constitutio* proves, none were more important
than the cities. The king has to promise to create
no more castles or cities on ecclesiastical lands—the
first step in the disintegration of the ecclesiastical
lordships and their absorption piecemeal into the
royal demesne. New—in other words, royal—markets must not compete with the older markets in
princely hands: travellers must not be compelled
to take the new roads and thus pay toll to the king
instead of the princes. More important are the
clauses which show that the royal officials had been

Weller, 234, in denying that the statute implied " die Schöpfung der
fürstlichen Landeshoheit," or that it increased the princes' powers, ap-
proximates to Niese's view.—For the text, cf. MG. *Const.* II, 211—213
(No. 171).
[33] Niese, 54; cf. Rosenstock, *op. cit.*, 411.

extending their jurisdiction to the detriment of princely courts, changing the seats of hundred-courts and (without doubt) centralizing them in the royal towns, and that the jurisdiction of royal cities had been extended " ultra civitatis ambitum ", absorbing and occupying the " proprietates et feoda " of nobles and churches. Every one of the twenty-three clauses—of which thirteen expressly refer to towns and markets—is a proof both of the growth and of the vitality of the principality which the Hohenstaufen had created in less than a century from the only moderately extensive demesnes which the civil wars had left to the crown. Every clause reveals the possibilities which this " state ", so little appreciated, possessed of becoming the nucleus of a new Germany. And every clause—this is perhaps the most notable feature of all—shows the nobility on the defensive, the crown, with the initiative firmly in its grasp, boldly setting out to be the predominant princely power in Germany, always attacking, always building, in spite of foreign and imperial preoccupations in masterly control of the German situation.

A proper understanding of the famous constitution of 1232 does nothing to diminish its importance. It was, without doubt, a check on the crown, a Magna Carta of princely liberties. But it is important nevertheless to see that it was directed not against the emperor in his imperial capacity, but against the successful territorial prince which not even his preoccupation with the struggle with Innocent IV and the Lombard cities could prevent Frederick II from being. The *constitutio in favorem principum* was not promulgated because Frederick, absorbed in Italy, was forced to leave Germany to the princes, but because he and his son were so intent on building up their *Hausmacht* in Germany that an opposition was evoked with which it was necessary at least to temporize. It is not our purpose to examine the political situation in which the constitution was promulgated; but it seems clear that Henry VII, whose abilities have been exaggerated,[34] had shown neither tact nor moderation in the pursuit of objects which, sound enough in themselves, demanded infinite patience and careful handling, and had roused, together with his " evil counsellors," an opposition as powerful as that which his English contemporary, Henry III, had to meet. It is hard to see how Frederick had any choice except to give way, particularly as, from a legal point of view, the princes had every reason to claim that Henry's government had gone far beyond the bounds of law. The pretexts of consanguinity and so forth, which princes like Henry the Lion and Otto of Wittelsbach never failed to bring forward to justify the absorption of fiefs and jurisdictions,[35] show how circumspectly territorial policy had to be framed; and it was precisely through lack of circumspection that Henry VII failed. There was no wisdom in riding roughshod over vested interests and, for the emperor, there could be no question of riding roughshod over legitimate rights. If the constitution of 1232 had been, as so many historians have maintained,

---

[34] This—whatever its other merits—must be the verdict on E. Franzel's stimulating study, *König Heinrich VII. v. Hohenstaufen. Studien z. Gesch. des " Staates " in Deutschland* (1929).

[35] The examples brought forward by Hildebrand and Spindler are too numerous to cite; but it is necessary to insist how right Spindler is (pp. 44, 99, etc.) in reducing the various " claims " which the dukes always managed to produce, to mere pretexts; cf. also Hildebrand, 218.—The same method, as is well known, was a cardinal feature of French policy, both at home and abroad, in the thirteenth century, and the care which the Capetians invariably took to frame a legal case was one reason for the prominence of jurists in French governmental circles; cf. Kern, *Ausdehnungspolitik*, 36—39.

" une sanction légale à beaucoup d'usurpations qui n'étaient jusqu'alors que des tolérances,"[36] there would be just grounds for considering the emperor's concessions as a surrender to princely egotism. But we have seen that the rights which the new princely class began to exercise in the twelfth century cannot be considered as usurpations,[37] and that if there is a question of usurpation and illegality, it is Henry VII's government which is at fault. Instead of localizing opposition by a slow and piecemeal process of gradual consolidation, Henry took up a challenging attitude which brought him face to face with a united opposition along the whole front; and against this frontal attack the Hohenstaufen could no more stand firm than any other princes. The son had put the father in a false position; and Frederick had no alternative except to withdraw.[38]

1232 was without doubt a year of crisis, but the concessions which the crown made that year marked no turning point, and three years later Frederick

[36] Blondel, *Politique de l'empereur Frédéric II en Allemagne*, 129.

[37] *Supra*, 102 sqq.

[38] If the constitutional position in 1232 has been considered at some length, it is because a majority of historians still consider that at this moment—which is regarded as a turning-point—Italian policy decisively influenced Frederick's actions; e.g., Rörig, *Partikularismus*, 11, or even Weller, *Städtegründung*, 234. That there is something to be said in support of this view, cannot be denied; but, as Hirsch has said (HG., 237), " solche Feststellungen sind nicht unrichtig, sie stellen aber doch nur die äussere Seite des Problems dar." In other words, the constitutional problem still remains; and even a historian who concludes that Frederick was thinking predominantly of Italian complications, cannot escape the further question, whether, the constitutional position being what it was, another solution was possible. The danger of emphasizing the Italian connexion, however, is precisely that—an easy solution having been found—it is tempting to omit the further question altogether. It leads also—as in Franzel's book and Rosenstock's essay—to a false contrast between the emperor and his son, in which Frederick is depicted as sacrificing Henry's true German policy to his own Italian schemes. In fact, the difference between the two is one of method alone; and an objective study suggests that Henry's methods were reckless and precipitate, and that there is something of the difference between him and his father which is found between Henry II of England and his sons.

was able to show that his had been a policy of *reculer pour mieux sauter*.[39] The subsequent annexation of Austria and Styria, which we have already mentioned, points the same way.[40] But the events of 1231 and 1232 show clearly where the main danger lay. It was not the royal or imperial rights and prerogatives which the princes attacked, but the principality which was the only means the Hohenstaufen possessed to transform their royal position, with its roots in an Ottonian world which was dead and a feudal world which was dying, into a " modern " kingship set above a " modern " state.[41] Success or failure depended on ability to develop the territory which we may call the " crown principality "—for it was no longer a mere demesne—until the " crown principality " and Germany became identical terms. The history of Germany was, in short, coupled with the history of the Hohenstaufen principality. Even after the extinction of the Hohenstaufen dynasty, it offered—under Rudolf of Habsburg—a real chance of territorial reconstruction and, joined with the Habsburg dynastic lands, was a fair basis for the building of a revived monarchy.[42] But, as we know, these possibilities did not materialize. Rudolf's death saw the end of the last great attempt to hold the " crown principality " together and to strengthen it by amalgamation with the lands of the ruling dynasty.[43] With the coming of the fourteenth century the monarchy was already an empty preroga-

---

[39] Blondel admits as much, pp. 129—130 (" Frédéric paraît, en effet, avoir tenté de poser les bases d'un développement nouveau . . .").

[40] *Supra*, 117.

[41] For the conception of the " modern " state in the Hohenstaufen period, cf. Th. Mayer, *infra* II, 178—179, 197—199.

[42] Cf. O. Redlich, *Rudolf v. Habsburg. Das deutsche Reich nach dem Untergange des alten Kaisertums* (1903), bk. III, c. 1.

[43] Niese, 34.

tive, without the solid and independent territorial
basis which alone could make it a reality. Imperial
rights still remained alive, the crown still had its
prerogatives;[44] but the lack of a strongly organized
territory with adequate material resources meant
inability to exploit them, and this in its turn led
to atrophy, loss and powerlessness.

In the last resort, therefore, all depended on the
territorium which the Hohenstaufen had welded
together. No doubt there were other influential
factors. The relations between the crown and the
feudal baronies outside the royal demesne were not
so favourable to a policy of "reintegration" as in
France. It was not simply that the Hohenstaufen
were later than the Capetians in organizing a strict
feudal hierarchy[45]—that by the time their work
could begin the rights of the vassalage were so firmly
established that they opposed an unbreakable barrier
to the strengthening of the corresponding rights of
the vassals' superior[46]—but rather that, in a very
different environment, they had to build on a very
different historical foundation.[47] There is, in the
first place, the transformation of the face of Germany
by new settlement and colonization, which resulted
not only in a vast extension of German boundaries—
" the great deed of the German people in the middle
ages ", wrote LAMPRECHT,[48] " was the recovery of
three-fifths of modern Germany from the Slavs "—

[44] Hirsch, HG., 237.
[45] On the inadequacy of this type of argument, cf. *infra* II, 9, 31.
[46] On the " polarity " within feudal law of the *Vasallenrecht* and the
Herrenrecht, cf. Mitteis, *infra* II, 278.
[47] Mayer's essay, *infra* II, 1—33, is the best survey of the organic
differences between the two lands, and emphasis is rightly placed on the
transformation of Germany by colonization, which was as effective constitutionally as economically.
[48] I quote from Thompson's translation (*Feudal Germany*, xviii).

but also in the rise of new constitutional forces and
a radical alteration in the balance of power.[49] The
east colonial lands, the duchy of Austria in particular,
now came to the fore, and the seat of political power
was moved from west to east. The older regions
round Rhine and Main no longer had the same
predominance, and the crown was forced to give
increasingly marked attention to the princes who
had built up a powerful position in the east. From
this point of view, Germany by the second half of the
twelfth or the first half of the thirteenth century,
had become a constitutional structure such as the
early middle ages could never have conceived. By
1235 Saxony had been replaced by the duchies of
Westphalia, Anhalt and Brunswick, and even earlier
Bavaria, which had lost Carinthia at the end of the
tenth century, had been reduced by the creation of
the independent duchies of Austria and Styria. It
is no accident that this sudden growth of new territorial units occurred in the colonial east;[50] but the
changes in west Germany, though less striking, were
not less real. There also, as MAYER has shown,[51]
internal colonization brought a new accession of
strength to the princes at the critical moment; and,

[49] Rosenstock, *Königshaus u. Stämme*, 109—119, has particularly
emphasized the rising constitutional significance of the colonial east:
for him the constitutional struggles of the twelfth century were a contest
between the " stem-lands " of the west and the " marcher lands " of the
east—a struggle for the replacement of the older organization and the
" personal " principle of government by the new idea of a consolidated
territorial state, which is so strikingly apparent in territories like Austria,
and which, in Rosenstock's view, developed from the special powers conferred on the *Markgrafen* for the defence of the borders. But there is no
doubt that the constitutional peculiarities of marcher organization in the
early period have been exaggerated (cf. Dopsch, *Verf.- u. Wirtschaftsgesch.*,
83) and were not pronounced enough to have this decisive result. Nor
can the contemporary growth of the new " territorial " principles of government in old west Germany—there is no sign of infiltration or borrowing—
be explained on this theory; cf. *infra* II, 25.
[50] *Infra* II, 192.
[51] *Infra* II, 24.

not the least of the difficulties which confronted the Hohenstaufen, was the fact that their endeavours to set the organization of the realm on a new basis coincided with what almost amounted to a revolutionary movement within the ranks of the German nobility.[52] At the same time the princely power with which the German rulers had to deal imposed on them a policy which was very different from that of the French monarchs. The Capetians of the twelfth century, it is well known, used the lesser baronage against the greater nobility. In Germany, on the other hand, the situation left by the civil wars under Henry IV and Henry V necessitated co-operation with the great princes against the " dynasts ": the new duchies were the instruments created by the Hohenstaufen and endowed with powers to curb the dynastic aristocracy.[53] However necessary this policy was, it cannot be denied that it involved an element of risk. If, in particular, the crown were unable to assert the same rights over its tenants-in-chief as the tenants-in-chief asserted over their vassals, if the current of power which rose through the feudal system from its broad foundation in the knightly class never reached the apex, royal supremacy must inevitably be threatened. And

[52] Mitteis, ZRG. *Germ. Abt.* LVII (1937), 574, rightly insists that, in spite of all that the Hohenstaufen undertook and attempted, the period has " den Charakter einer fast revolutionären Bewegung im Hochadel . . . und die Fürsten als die eigentlich treibenden Faktoren erscheinen." This is clear, for example, at the time of the fall of Henry the Lion, when the whole constitutional situation appears to be based on compromise; cf. Niese, HZ. CXII (1914), 555, and *infra* II, 260.

[53] *Supra*, 102—108.—Hirsch, MIÖG. XXXV (1914), 85 n. 2, rightly points out that this situation inevitably involved the crown in inconsistencies. On the one side, there was naturally a tendency for the king to support the counts and the higher nobility—" wo es anging "—against the rising duchies. On the other, they were compelled to evince " Entgegenkommen gegen die Territorialfürsten." These were conflicting tendencies, " zwischen denen die königliche Gewalt durchzukommen hatte, und die nicht aus einem einheitlichen Plane, den man dann Staatsreform nennen müsste, erklärt werden können."

precisely such a differentiation between crown and princes has been seen in the peculiarly German institution, the *Leihezwang*.[54]   If the king were to be forced to grant out every barony which escheated to the crown, to grant it out undivided and unimpaired, a check was set on the " reintegration " of the realm by a process of absorption into the " crown principality ".   And precisely this was the principle of *Leihezwang*—a principle which was alive and vigorous in 1180, if not before.[55]   But, however vigorous, it was not then, or for three generations more, an accepted principle of German law.[56]   We have already seen that Henry VI overrode it in 1191 and 1195 and that Frederick II—who expressly repudiated it in 1227[57]—did likewise in 1237 and 1246[58].   Nor was Frederick's death a turning point in this regard. Even William of Holland insisted on his freedom to dispose of escheats: if, he wrote in 1252, princes and barons failed to do homage within a year and a day for their fiefs, " omnia illa feuda et principatus nobis vacaverunt et vacant et de illis possumus disponere secundum quod nobis placuerit, retinendo nobis vel aliis in feudum concedendo."[59]

These facts are important because they show that, even in this regard, the turning point did not come until after 1250.   Compared with France, the Hohenstaufen may well have had a difficult task to accomplish; but until and even after Frederick II's death the crucial moment had not been reached at which long-lived and deeply-rooted tendencies—

---

[54] On the *Leihezwang*, cf. Mitteis, *infra* II, 249, 259, 276.

[55] Mitteis, *Lr. u. Sg.*, 692 sqq.

[56] *Ibid.*, 698—700, where the material is assembled; cf. Kienast, HZ. CLVIII (1938), 14.

[57] Cf. MG. *Const.* II, 152 (No. 116).

[58] *Supra*, 117.

[59] MG. *Const.* II, 466 (No. 359).

I

none of which is more remarkable than the *Leihe-zwang*—had been transformed into immutable laws and customs of the constitution. There was nothing which a monarchy with a firm territorial basis and a consciousness of its own territorial power could not still ultimately overcome.[60] Once again, therefore, we come back to the Hohenstaufen *territorium*— this time with a clear realization that their failure was a failure to build up a territory which could outlive themselves and provide a sure basis for the monarchy, whoever wielded monarchical power. For this was, in the end, the cause of the disintegration of late mediaeval Germany. If the Staufen lands had remained, after Frederick's death, the strong, highly-organized territory which he made them during his life, the situation would still have had great potentialities for his successors, and the electoral college, which now came to rule the destinies of the German monarchy,[61] might have been reduced again to a position no stronger than that of the " Pairs de France ".[62]

What was necessary, in the first place, was an administration which would function as well without the king as under his supervision. Necessary also was loyalty and solidarity among the inhabitants. But neither the one nor the other had been achieved. The beginnings were, indeed, there—strongly in evidence, for example, in the League of Rhenish Cities which strove to maintain the principles of

[60] Cf. Kienast, HZ. CLVIII, 9.

[61] Cf. particularly M. Krammer, *Das Kurfürstenkolleg von seinen Anfängen bis z. Zusammenschluss im Renser Kurverein d. J.* 1338 (1913), and the texts in the same author's *Quellen z. Gesch. d. deutschen Königswahl u. des Kurfürstenkollegs* (2nd ed., 1918).—Cf. further H. Mitteis, *Die deutsche Königswahl. Ihre Rechtsgrundlagen bis zur goldenen Bulle* (1938).

[62] For a brief comparison of the German *Kurfürstenkolleg* and the *Pairs de France*, cf. Schramm, ZRG. Kan. Abt. XXVI, 179.

Hohenstaufen government through the Interregnum[63] —and they provided, as we have seen, a basis which Rudolf of Habsburg could use on his accession in 1273. But the Hohenstaufen had not time to create a lasting "state" within the state. We have tried to show how mistaken it is to attempt to explain the failure of the German monarchy to establish its position by accidents like the early death of Henry VI or complications—serious though they were—like the struggles with Gregory VII, Alexander III or Innocent IV. The constitutional life of a nation cannot, as ROSENSTOCK so clearly perceived, be interpreted simply as the result of chance, lawlessness, abuse and usurpation.[64] But the position of the territorial prince was very different from that of the monarch, and the Hohenstaufen, we must never forget, were territorial princes as well as sovereigns. It was in their princely capacity, not in their royal capacity, that they were really vulnerable. As princes they had, in the first place, no special position : the sacred majesty of kingship, which though intangible was potent and vividly alive, could not hide the purely local character of their territorial policy or save it from the opposition of the other local powers whose aims and objects were identical. Of this fact the events of 1231 and 1232 are clear proof : those who, like the ecclesiastical princes, had no thought of attacking the imperial rights of their sovereign rulers, were prepared to attack and to beat down, if possible, their princely power. In the second place, the principality which the Hohenstaufen moulded into shape was a new creation without a long tradition of government to hold it together.

[63] Cf. E. Bielfeldt, *Der Rheinische Bund. v.* 1254. *Ein erster Versuch einer Reichsreform* (1937).
[64] *Königshaus u. Stämme,* v–vi; cf. similarly Hirsch, HG., 211.

In these circumstances, casual events, accidents and setbacks assume an importance which they can never obtain in the history of Germany as a whole. It is only necessary to open the history of Brunswick, Bavaria, Austria, or any of the principalities, great or small, lay or ecclesiastical, at random to see how largely their fortune depends on fortuitous deaths, lucky marriages, petty alliances, personal capacity;[65] and to this rule the Hohenstaufen state was, and could be, no exception. The Wittelsbach power in Bavaria, for example, was built on the accident— for no explanation and no combination of explanations is sufficient to account for it—that all the dynastic aristocracy of the land perished without direct heirs in the course of the thirteenth century.[66] The accidents which affected the Hohenstaufen tended from the beginning the other way. Barbarossa, we have seen, had acquired Regensburg as a solid pillar of his territorial position in the south-east;[67] but the early death of his sons Frederick (in 1191) and Otto (in 1201) and the struggle between Philip of Swabia and Otto of Brunswick after Henry VI's death in 1197 robbed the victory of permanence, and by 1205 the prefect of Regensburg was an official, not of the Hohenstaufen, but of the Wittelsbach dukes of Bavaria.[68]   And this example is but one of many. The dissipation of imperial lands under Philip of Swabia, even if exaggerated,[69] is well known.

[65] Cf. *infra* II, 30.
[66] Spindler, 12; cf. *infra* II, 275. The position in Austria was similar; Dopsch, *Verf.- u. Wirtschaftsgesch.*, 83.
[67] *Supra*, 114.
[68] Spindler, 17—18.
[69] Cf. Schneider, *Elsass*, 144; Niese, *Verwaltung*, 56; Klewitz, *Ministerialität*, 60; Weller, *Städtegründung*, 192.—Eberhardt, *Nordthüringen*, 40, suggests with considerable probability that, as Philip of Swabia's efforts to maintain the demesne are clear beyond doubt, the responsibility for dissipation of the fisc appears to lie with Otto of Brunswick.

A decade like that which followed Henry VI's death could work havoc in a principality which was in the process of formation and consolidation, composed of heterogenous lands and rights with a constant tendency to break apart and revert to their older attachments, needing above all a continuous and tranquil rule in which a durable tradition could be created.

Fifty years could not create a state which would stand ten years of anarchy, any more than ten years of anarchy could destroy—though they might impair—a constitutional organism like Germany or an institution like the monarchy, which together had stood the stress of centuries. That, in the end, is the difference between the position of the Hohenstaufen as kings and their position as princes. Shocks like the interregnum of 1198—1212 and of 1250—1273, which—as the reigns of Frederick II and, on a lesser scale, of Rudolf of Habsburg show— could not undermine the main principles of monarchical government and could not destroy the traditions on which the monarchy was built, were fatal to a territory which was in the process of becoming, but was not yet, a consolidated state. Personal control, continuity, and strict supervision were needed to prevent the ministerial class adopting the interests of the baronage and being absorbed into the lesser nobility. Such control was lacking in the Hohenstaufen territory at the crucial moments. It is clear that the years 1198—1212 saw the transformation of offices into fiefs;[70] and though Frederick II, as we have seen,[71] checked this tendency, it came to the fore again after his death, or even earlier as a result

[70] Niese, 198.
[71] *Supra*, 116.

of the attack on the emperor at the Council of Lyons. When Frederick II appointed his *ministerialis*, Philip of Falkenstein, to be *procurator* in the Wetterau, his act marked a stage in the development of a dependent administration;[72] but the Falkenstein family quickly adopted the outlook of the old nobility, transformed its office into a feudal county,[73] and was busy, as early as 1309, in building up its feudal authority over the neighbouring villages.[74] In the same way the stronghold of Landskrone was in the hands of the *ministerialis*, Gerhard of Sinzig, at the time of Frederick II's death; and although he was already calling himself *dominus de Landscrone* in 1248, it was the Interregnum which saw the final disuse of the family name, and in the next generation the former *ministerialis* had become a lord with an independent lordship.[75] The same process is evident elsewhere, at Kaiserswerth, Dortmund and Aachen, for example.[76] Other princes met the danger by taking power out of ministerial hands and transferring it to a real official class;[77] but—in spite of the fact that the Hohenstaufen were far from solely dependent on ministerial servants[78]—the opportunity to uproot the growing power of the *ministeriales* never came, and where other princes were busy introducing a more modern bureaucracy, the Hohenstaufen were necessarily more bent on repairing the damage to their

---

[72] *Infra* II, 224.
[73] Niese, 38.
[74] *Ibid.*, 64 n. 8.
[75] *Ibid.*, 256. Cf. Aubin, *Landeshoheit*, 410, and for the further history of the Sinzig family, who eventually became vassals of the counts of Jülich, cf. v. Gladiss, *Beiträge z. Gesch. d. staufischen Reichsministerialität* (1934), 102 sqq.
[76] Niese, 166–7.
[77] Cf. for example Klewitz, *Hildesheim*, 37, Spindler, 149—150, and particularly Aubin, 407—415.
[78] Cf. v. Gladiss, 62, Niese, 141, 145 sqq.

older organization which periods like the decade after the death of Henry VI were bound to engender. The Interregnum of 1250—1273 therefore found the *ministeriales* strongly entrenched in an independent position, and the natural result was that, through lack of a superior power which could hold it together, the principality which the Hohenstaufen had built broke apart into a mass of petty lordships, castellanies, territories and towns—the most disjointed region of late mediaeval Germany. This failure was a territorial failure and disruption came from within. But it was a failure which involved the whole of Germany as well. The central provinces, which were the core around which the whole land might have been assembled, became the land with so many lords that it was in essence lordless. Without the central core, however, the greater states in north and east had perforce to go their own way and to fulfil a destiny which was provincial rather than national, Saxon or Bavarian and not German. It was the failure of the central member of the great feudal confederation which had been formed in Barbarossa's reign that condemned Germany, for many subsequent centuries, to decentralization and disunion.

The failure of the Hohenstaufen territory is not difficult to explain. External causes, of which there were plenty, were sufficient to destroy the beginnings which had been made. The growth and formation of the German territories was a process which took centuries of slow consolidation to complete,[79] and the Hohenstaufen had at most three generations in which to work. It was not long enough to produce a durable

[79] Cf. the excellent paragraph in Rörig, *Partikularismus*, 20—22, and in general H. Spangenberg, *Vom Lehnstaat zum Ständestaat* (1912).

result. And without the Hohenstaufen principality which, as we have seen, was the centre round which feudal Germany was to crystallize into a unified state, the predominance of the monarchy was destroyed. It is easy to see an end of imperial sovereignty in 1250. But not even the princes themselves, who are supposed to have profited most from the break up, realized that the end had come or sought to prevent Rudolf of Habsburg from " revindicating " imperial rights. Imperial rights were there, at the end of the thirteenth century, if they could have been used to effect, and in Germany, as in Italy, if there were princely egotists,[80] there was also a by no means negligible party which looked to a restoration of imperial government as the main end of political life. But with every year that passed, the empire became more of a memory, its rights mere shadows, its authority a phantom, which neither Charles IV, Sigismund nor Maximilian I could revive. The collapse of the royal territory, on which the Hohenstaufen had expended so much of their energy, had been the cause of German disintegration, and the lack of a royal territory was the cause of its continuance. The concentration of the Hohenstaufen on their own demesne is often regarded as an acknowledgement of defeat, a beginning of the end. In fact, we have seen that it was not only the sole policy which was practicable after the defeat of Henry IV and the nullification of his policy by the dynastic opposition, but also a policy rich in hope and potentialities. The Germany it foresaw was a federation of principalities, tied to the crown by strong feudal bonds. But for such a policy a strong royal territory was essential; and when that failed, the rest inevitably went to

[80] Rörig, 19.

pieces. The disintegrating tendencies of feudalism, which had always been strong in Germany as compared with France, came to the fore; the electoral principle, combated until the very end of Hohenstaufen times, became a tenet of constitutional law; the allegiance of the princes was based not on respect for a monarch who was powerful enough to make his supreme authority felt, but on compromises, capitulations and promises. All these tendencies the Hohenstaufen had held in check: all of them took force when the essential territorial basis of government was torn away. But there was none of them which, in 1250, was so embedded in constitutional life that it could not have been eradicated, if it had been possible to build a durable crown principality or to hand on unimpaired to a new line of rulers the principality which the Hohenstaufen had formed. But that principality was not well enough established to become a permanent element in constitutional life. Three generations of building had set it up: three more, at least, were needed to set it on a durable foundation. But a durable foundation was never secured. Not the royal principality, but the seven electoral principalities became the keystone of the constitution, and there was no independent royal power to hold the balance. When that result, already implicit in the events of 1338, was confirmed by the Golden Bull of 1356, the last shadow of the Hohenstaufen constitution had passed away, and Germany was set on the long and broken course which led by slow and painful steps to 1870.

INDEX

Advocacy, 65–70, 96–97, 119.
Alexander III, 103.
Alsace, 114, 120.
Altenburg, 113—114.
Anhalt, duchy of, 127.
Arnulf, East Frankish King, 29.
Arnulf, duke of Bavaria, 30, 38, 49.
Austria, duchy of, 45, 103, 105, 117, 125, 127.
Austria, dukes of: cf. Babenberger, Habsburger.

Babenberger, dukes of Austria, 106.
Bamberg, bishopric of, 61, 64.
Bannleihe, 97.
Bavaria, 31, 38, 40, 42, 45, 112.
Bavaria, dukes of; cf. Arnulf, Eberhard, Henry the Lion, Otto of Wittelsbach.
Bern, 120.
Beromünster, mon. of, 69.
Berthold I of Zähringen, 43.
Billunger, dukes of Saxony, 42.
Black Forest, 119.
Bohemia, 30.
Bouvines, battle of, 11, 13.
Bremen, archbishopric of, 64.
Bruno, archbishop of Cologne, 71.
Brunswick, duchy of, 127.
Burchard, duke of Swabia, 37.
Burggraf, 116.

Calixtus II, 99—100.
Carinthia, 30, 42, 127.
Carolingian constitution, 4, 24, 66.
Castellany (*Burgbezirk*), 82, 85, 116.
Chancery, organisation of, 71.
Charles Martel, 29.
Charles the Great (Charlemagne), 29, 88.
Cistercian order, 98, 106.
Clement II, 75.
Clovis, Frankish King, 29.
Cluny, mon. of, 62.
Cologne, archbishops of; cf. Bruno.
Colonization, 96, 105, 118, 126—127.
Concordat of Worms, 10, 65, 98—101.

Conrad I, 30—32, 36.
Conrad II, 55, 62, 80.
Conrad III, 56, 58.
Constitutio in favorem principum, 120—122.
Coronation (royal), 38, 52—53.
County organization, 80, 83, 87.
Criminal justice, 66, 84, 87, 96—97, 105.

Demesne, royal (crown lands), 6, 18, 37—38, 72, 85, 109, 115, 120—121, 132.
Devolution, right of, 87.
Dynasts; cf. High Nobility.

Eberhard, archbishop of Salzburg, 103.
Eberhard, duke of Bavaria, 38.
Eberhard, duke of Franconia, 32, 51.
Egerland, 113.
Eigenkirche; cf. Proprietary church system.
Eike von Repgow, 13.
Election (royal), 32, 49, 51—59.
Electoral princes (*Kurfürsten*), 130.
England, comparison with Germany, 5, 10, 13—20, 47, 109.
Eticho, 90—91.

Feudalism, 16, 102, 109—111, 126, 137.
Forchheim 48, 57.
France, comparison with Germany, 5, 16—17, 18—20, 28, 109—111, 117, 126, 128.
Franconia, 40, 42, 113—114;
Franconia, dukes of; cf. Eberhard.
Frederick I (Barbarossa), 76—79, 82, 87, 101—104, 106—107, 109, 113—114.
Frederick II, 6, 18—19, 23, 103, 106, 116, 120, 122—124, 129, 133—134.

Gerhard of Sinzig (*dominus de Landscrone*), 134.